FREEDOM TO RO

D1459442

South Pennines
and the
Brontë Moors

INCLUDING ILKLEY MOOR

South Pennines
and the
Bronte Moors

INCLUDING ILKLEY MOOR

Andrew Bibby

The Ramblers

FRANCES LINCOLN

FREEDOM TO ROAM

The Freedom to Roam guides
are dedicated to the memory of
Benny Rothman

Frances Lincoln Ltd, 4 Torriano Mews, Torriano Avenue, London NW5 2RZ
www.franceslincoln.com

South Pennines and the Bronte Moors
Copyright © Andrew Bibby 2005

All photographs except those on pages 97 and 119 © John Morrison
Photograph on page 97 by Andy Hey © rspb-images.com; photograph on page 119
from the original painting *A Chartist Meeting, Basin Stones, Todmorden 1842* by
Aldred W. Bayes (1831–1901) © Mark Croft; illustration on page 38 © Edward
Vickerman, Ilkley Archaeology Group; illustration on page 137 © David Langworth;
illustration on page 144 © Martin Bagness

Lyrics from 'The Manchester Rambler' song by Ewan MacColl used by kind permission
of Peggy Seeger and of the publisher Harmony Music Ltd

Maps reproduced from Ordnance Survey mapping on behalf of The Controller
of Her Majesty's Stationery Office © Crown Copyright 100043293 2004

First published by Frances Lincoln 2005

British Library Cataloguing in Publication Data
A catalogue record for this book is available from the British Library

ISBN 0 7112 2501 X
Printed and bound in Singapore by Kyodo Printing Co.
9 8 7 6 5 4 3 2 1

Frontispiece photograph: Bride Stones, near Todmorden

Contents

Acknowledgments

The author gratefully acknowledges the assistance given him by a wide range of individuals and organizations, and is particularly grateful for the help offered by Kate Conto and Dan French of the Ramblers' Association, Kate Cave and Fiona Robertson at Frances Lincoln, Gwen Goddard, Tim Melling (RSPB), David Parsons (City of Bradford Countryside Service), Harold Sculthorpe, Alan Gaskell, Elsie Gaskell, Will Sutcliffe, Margaret Rooker, Maureen Ludlam, Arnold Kellett, Edward Vickerman, Mark Croft, Roly Smith, Richard Peters, Nigel Smith, Richard Blakeley, John Crummett, Steve Hall, Anne Hoggarth, Moira Atkinson and Jane Scullion.

Series introduction

This book, and the companion books in the series, celebrate the arrival in England and Wales of the legal right to walk in open country. The title for the series is borrowed from a phrase much used during the long campaign for this right – Freedom to Roam. For years, it was the dream of many to be able to walk at will across mountain top, moorland and heath, free of the risk of being confronted by a 'Keep Out' sign or being turned back by a gamekeeper.

The sense of frustration that the hills were, in many cases, out of bounds to ordinary people was captured in the song 'The Manchester Rambler', which was written by one of the best-known figures in Britain's post-war folk revival, Ewan MacColl. The song, which was inspired by the 1932 'mass trespass' on Kinder Scout when walkers from Sheffield and Manchester took to the forbidden Peak District hills, tells the tale of an encounter between a walker, trespassing on open land, and an irate gamekeeper:

> *He called me a louse, and said 'Think of the grouse',*
> *Well I thought but I still couldn't see*
> *Why old Kinder Scout, and the moors round about*
> *Couldn't take both the poor grouse and me.*

The desire, as Ewan MacColl expressed it, was a simple one:

> *So I'll walk where I will, over mountain and hill*
> *And I'll lie where the bracken is deep,*
> *I belong to the mountains, the clear running fountains*
> *Where the grey rocks rise ragged and steep.*

Some who loved the outdoors and campaigned around the time of the Kinder Scout trespass in the 1930s must have thought that the legal right to walk in open country would be won after the Second World War, at the time when the National Parks were being created and the rights-of-way network drawn up. It was not to be. It was another half century before, finally, Parliament passed the Countryside and Rights of Way Act 2000, and the people of England and Wales gained the legal right to take to the hills and the moors. (Scotland has its own traditions and its own legislation.)

We have dedicated this series to the memory of Benny Rothman, one of the leaders of the 1932 Kinder Scout mass trespass who was imprisoned for his part in what was deemed a 'riotous assembly'. Later in his life, Benny Rothman was a familiar figure at rallies called by the Ramblers' Association as once again the issue of access rights came to the fore. But we should pay tribute to all who have campaigned for this goal. Securing greater access to the countryside was one of the principles on which the Ramblers' Association was founded in 1935, and for many ramblers the access legislation represents the achievement of literally a lifetime of campaigning.

So now, at last, we do have freedom to roam. For the first time in several centuries, the open mountains, moors and heaths of England and Wales are legally open for all. We have the protected right to get our boots wet in the peat bogs, to flounder in the tussocks, to blunder and scrabble through the bracken and heather, and to discover countryside which, legally, we had no way of knowing before.

The Freedom to Roam series of books has one aim: to encourage you to explore and grow to love these new areas of the countryside which are now open to us. The right to roam freely – that's surely something to celebrate.

Walking in open country – a guide to using this book

If the right and the freedom to roam openly are so important – perceptive readers may be asking – why produce a set of books to tell you where to go?

So a word of explanation about this series. The aim is certainly not to encourage walkers to follow each other ant-like over the hills, sticking rigidly to a pre-determined itinerary. We are not trying to be prescriptive, instructing you on your walk stile by stile or gate by gate. The books are not meant as instruction manuals but we hope that they will be valuable as *guides* – helping you discover areas of the countryside which you haven't legally walked on before, advising you on routes you might want to take and telling you about places of interest on the way.

In areas where it can be tricky to find routes or track down landmarks, we offer more detailed instructions.

Elsewhere, we are deliberately less precise in our directions, allowing you to choose your own path or line to follow. For each walk, however, there is a recommended core route, and this forms the basis on which the distances given are calculated.

There is, then, an assumption that those who use this book will be comfortable with using a map – and that, in practice, means one of the Ordnance Survey's 1:25 000 Explorer series of maps. As well as using the maps in this book, it is worth taking the full OS map with you, to give a wider picture of the countryside you will be exploring.

Safety in the hills

Those who already are experienced upland walkers will not be surprised if at this point we put in a note on

basic safety in the hills.
Walkers need to remember
that walking in open country,
particularly high country,
is different from footpath
walking across farmland
or more gentle countryside.
The main risk is of being
inadequately prepared for
changes in weather. Even in
high summer, hail and even
snow are not impossible.
Daniel Defoe found this out in
August 1724 when he crossed
the Pennines from Rochdale,
leaving a calm clear day
behind to find himself
almost lost in a blizzard on
the tops.

If rain comes, temperatures
will drop, so it is important
when taking to the hills to
be properly equipped and to
guard against the risk of
hypothermia. Fortunately,
walkers today have access to
a range of wind- and rain-
proof clothing which was not
available in the eighteenth
century. Conversely, in
hot weather, take sufficient
water to avoid the risk
of dehydration and
hyperthermia (dangerous

overheating of the body).

Be prepared for visibility to
drop, when (to use the local
term) the clag descends on
the hills. It is always sensible
to take a compass. If you
are unfamiliar with basic
compass-and-map work, ask
in a local outdoor equipment
shop whether they have
simple guides available or
pick the brains of a more
experienced walker.

The other main hazard,
even for walkers who know
the hills well, is that of
suffering an accident such as
a broken limb. If you plan to
walk alone, it is sensible to
let someone know in advance
where you will be walking
and when you expect to be
back – the moorland and
mountain rescue services
which operate in the areas
covered by this book are very
experienced but they are not
psychic. Groups of walkers
should tackle only what the
least experienced or least fit
member of the party can
comfortably achieve. Take
particular care if you intend
to take children with you to

hill country. And take a mobile phone by all means, but don't assume you can rely on it in an emergency, since some parts of the moors and hills will not pick up a signal. (If you can make a call and are in a real emergency situation, ring 999 – it is the police who coordinate mountain and moorland rescues.)

If this sounds off-putting, that is certainly not the intention. The guiding principle behind the access legislation is that walkers will exercise their new-won rights with responsibility. Taking safety precautions is just one aspect of acting responsibly.

Access land – what you can and can't do

Countryside covered by access legislation includes mountain, moor, heath, downland and common land. After the passing of the Countryside and Rights of Way Act 2000, a lengthy mapping process was undertaken, culminating in the production of 'conclusive' maps which identify land open for access. These maps (although not intended as guides for walking) can be accessed via the Internet, at www.countrysideaccess.gov.uk. Ordnance Survey maps published from 2004 onwards also show access land.

Note: Each walk has been graded, on a scale of 🥾 to 🥾 🥾 🥾 🥾 🥾 , for the degree of difficulty involved. In general, walks are judged more difficult if they are (a) longer in mileage, and/or (b) involve more rough walking (across open moorland rather than on established footpaths), and/or (c) pose more navigational problems or venture into very unfrequented areas. But bear in mind that all the walks in this book require map-reading competence and some experience of hill walking.

You can walk, run, birdwatch and climb on access land, although there is no new right to camp or to bathe in streams or lakes (or, of course, to drive vehicles). Dogs can come too, but the regulations sensibly insist that they are on leads near livestock and during the bird-nesting season (1 March to 31 July). Some grouse moors can ban dogs altogether, so watch out for local signs. Access legislation also does not include the right to ride horses or bikes, though in some areas there may be pre-existing agreements which allow this. More information is available on the website given above and, at the time

of writing, there is an advice line 0845 100 3298.

The access legislation allows for some open country to be permanently excluded from the right to roam. 'Excepted' land includes military land, quarries and areas close to buildings; in addition landowners can apply for other open land to be excluded. For example, at the time of writing, a number of areas of moorland which are used as rifle ranges have been designated in this way (these are not in areas covered by the walks described in this book).

To the best of the authors' knowledge, all the walks in the Freedom to Roam series

Twelve Apostles, Ilkley Moor

WALKING IN OPEN COUNTRY

are either on legal rights of way or across access land included in the official 'conclusive' maps. However, you are asked to bear in mind that the books have been produced right at the beginning of the new access arrangements, before walkers have begun regularly to walk the hills and before any teething problems on the ground have been ironed out. For instance, at the time of writing there were still some places where entry arrangements to access land had not been finalized. As access becomes better established, minor changes to the routes suggested may become appropriate or necessary. You are asked to remember that we are encouraging you to be flexible in the way you use these guides.

Walkers in open country also need to be aware that landowners have a further right to suspend or restrict access on their land for up to twenty-eight days a year. (In such cases of temporary closure, there will normally continue to be access on public holidays and on most weekends.) Notice of closure needs to be given in advance, and the plan is that this information should be readily available to walkers, it is hoped at local information centres and libraries but also on the countryside access website and at popular entry points to access land. This sort of set-up has generally worked well in Scotland, where arrangements have been put in place to make sure that walkers in areas where deer hunting takes place can find out exactly when and where hunting is happening.

Walkers will understand the sense in briefly closing small areas of open countryside when, for example, shooting is in progress (grouse shooting begins on 12 August) or when heather burning is taking place in spring. However, it is once again too early in the implementation of the access legislation to know how easily walkers in England and Wales will be able to find out about these temporary access closures. It is also too early to know whether landowners will attempt to abuse this power.

In some circumstances additional restrictions to access can be introduced – for example, on the grounds of nature conservation or heritage conservation, on the advice of English Nature and English Heritage.

Bear these points in mind, but enjoy your walking in the knowledge that any access restrictions should be the exception and not the norm. The Countryside Agency has itself stated that 'restrictions will be kept to a minimum'. If you do find access unexpectedly denied while walking in the areas suggested in this book, please accept the restrictions and follow the advice you are given. However, if you feel that access was wrongly denied, please report your experience to the countryside service of the local authority (or National Park authority, in National Park areas), and to the Ramblers' Association.

Finally, there may be occasions when you choose not to exercise your freedom to roam. For example, many of the upland moors featured in these books are the homes of ground-nesting birds such as grouse, curlew, lapwing and pipit, who will be building their nests in spring and early summer. During this time, many people will decide to leave the birds in peace and find other places to walk. Rest assured that you will know if you are approaching an important nesting area – birds are good at telling you that they would like you to go away.

Celebrating the open countryside

Despite these necessary caveats, the message from this series is, we hope, clear. Make the most of the new legal rights we have been given – and enjoy your walking.

Introduction

There may be no mountains in the south Pennines – or, at least, no mountains of the big, craggy kind you can find in the Scottish Highlands, the Lake District or Snowdonia – but this is certainly upland country. There are broad stretches of open moorland described in this book where it is easy to get away from other human beings, though you will find that you are still sharing the countryside with others: with the red grouse, with the curlew with its curved beak and distinctive cry, with the larks and the little pipits, and perhaps also with the grubby Pennine sheep, which the poet Ted Hughes once memorably described as 'the sluttiest sheep in England'.

The moors are not empty of life, but they can give that impression. This is a landscape which seems to be in need of adjectives such as desolate, or wild, or bleak. Indeed, the south Pennine moors can be wild places, particularly in winter when the snow is tumbling but in summer, too, when the rain lashes down or when dense white cloud reduces visibility.

These, after all, are what (thanks to some adroit marketing by somebody) we are increasingly coming to call the Bronte Moors. This is the landscape which serves as the backdrop to the drama of Emily Bronte's *Wuthering Heights* and the other novels written by the Bronte sisters during their time in Haworth, when they lived in the parsonage beside the graveyard close to the moor edge. The power of these novels comes in part at least from the vividness with which the moorland countryside is described. The brooding Heathcliff at Wuthering Heights, his storm-swept hilltop house, can seem to re-create perfectly the mood of the landscape in this part of northern England.

But a note of caution is needed here. Too much emphasis on wilderness or on Bronte-esque desolation gives a somewhat misleading picture. It is wrong to imagine, for example, that this is a primeval landscape untouched by human intervention. In fact, the south Pennine moorland landscape has changed considerably over the centuries, as a result partly of climate change but also of human activity. Today, thanks to a number of factors including overgrazing by livestock, the moorland tops are to a large extent barren of trees. But previously there was much more tree cover on the high ground, and the remains of tree trunks lodged in the peat bogs, which you may stumble across in your walks, are still there to remind us of the fact.

It is also not the case that the moors are places which humans have always tended to avoid. Just the opposite, in fact. Until recent times, human settlements in this part of the Pennines tended to be on the hills rather than in valley bottoms. For example it is high-up Heptonstall, not neighbouring Hebden Bridge, which is the original settlement in that part of the Calder valley. Hebden Bridge, and other valley-bottom communities, only began to be developed with the coming of the Industrial Revolution in the late eighteenth century.

Settlements such as Heptonstall, admittedly, were not built right on the moor itself. But go back further, to the earliest of times, and there is ample evidence that humans made their homes on what is now the high moorland. The first two walks in this book focus on Rombalds Moor, the generic name for the moors south of Ilkley and the place to go for some of the richest prehistoric carvings in Britain. Anyone who has seen, say, the Swastika Stone or the Badger Stone, or who has stood right at the highest part of the moor in the prehistoric Twelve Apostles stone circle, will begin to understand that the moors have been home to humans for several millennia. Stone Age artefacts have also come to light in other moorland areas visited by walks in this book – on windy Great Manshead Hill (Walk 11), for example, and on Midgley Moor (Walk 9).

In medieval times, too, the moors were vital in providing communication links between settlements. The transport arteries from one community to another avoided as much as possible the valley bottoms, where the ground was undrained,

boggy and potentially hazardous. Travellers sometimes needed to cross rivers at bridges or fords, but whenever they could they stayed on higher ground. For visitors who come to the south Pennines today, one of the distinctive elements of the

Keighley Moor

local landscape is the paved packhorse paths, known locally as causey-paths or causeways, which criss-cross the high hills. In the most apparently remote parts of the moors, it's possible to find stretches of paved path or little stone markers half-hidden under the vegetation. It's worth remembering that the trans-Pennine M62 is simply the latest transport link to be built across these hills.

The hills have also been a place of economic activity. In several areas visited by walks in this book the land has been worked for the wealth that can be found beneath it: most obviously, stone has been extracted from quarries to build the houses people needed for shelter, and to create the miles and miles of dry-stone walling which are another feature of the local landscape. One walk in this book, that to Hoof Stones Height (Walk 8), goes close to the old limestone 'hushings', where, with great effort, limestone was separated from other rock and vegetation and turned into much-needed lime.

This region of northern England can claim to be the cradle of the Industrial Revolution. Partly this was the consequence of the area's early history of cloth production (particularly spinning and handloom weaving) and the development, from around the sixteenth century, of a 'dual economy', in which families earned income from both farming and weaving. The topography of the area was also important for its early industrialization: streams tumbling down the cloughs (as the valleys are called here) provided the power to drive the early mills. Walkers with an interest in industrial archaeology will enjoy discovering the remains of mills built quite high up streams in what are open moorland areas – as, for example, on the upper stretches of the brook in Cragg Vale south of Mytholmroyd (Walks 10 and 11). Those with an interest in social history will know that they share these hills with the shades of the Chartists (see pages 118–121). Perhaps it's not so far-fetched to suggest that a book such as E.P. Thompson's classic

The Making of the English Working Class is just as appropriate as an introduction to the south Pennines as the novels of the Bronte sisters.

Industry of a different kind reached these hills in the later nineteenth century and had a major effect on the landscape. The rapidly expanding industrial towns of Lancashire and Yorkshire needed adequate sources of drinking water, and tremendous engineering works took place on the moors to create the reservoirs which could provide this. One by one, they took their place in the landscape and on the maps: Widdop and the Gorple reservoirs, Watersheddles, the Walshaw chain, Cant Clough, Withens Clough, Green Withens, Baitings and all the others which continue to contribute today to the supply of fresh water to this part of northern England. The engineering works (which continued until after the Second World War) were not limited to the reservoirs themselves, but included a network of tunnels to carry water which run for many miles deep under the moors. Occasional air shafts from these tunnels are a sign, to the observant, of their presence.

The upland moors of the south Pennines today remain a place of economic activity, though this fact can sometimes be forgotten. The moors may not be farmed in a conventional sense but they are nevertheless managed, for grouse shooting is a business. Grouse are wild birds but they are also carefully cosseted, and on the best-maintained grouse moors the heather is regularly burned back in the spring to provide the birds with the habitat they like best.

Shooting and nature conservation may seem unlikely partners, but both take place here. Gamekeepers earn their living from the moors, but so too do a growing number of naturalists and conservation officers, working for bodies such as English Nature and the RSPB. The south Pennines do not have National Park status but vast sections of the moors have been formally declared to be Sites of Special Scientific Interest and almost the whole south Pennine moorland has European status as a Special Protection Area.

If humans have, for millennia, shaped and worked these hills, underneath them all lies a geological inheritance which can be summed up in the two words 'millstone grit'. As is well known, the Pennine chain in Derbyshire and Yorkshire actually comprises two major rock types, the limestone which is predominant in the Yorkshire Dales and the White Peak area of the Peak District, and millstone grit which predominates in the part in between. In the north, the divide between limestone and gritstone is the boundary followed by this book: the border is roughly the Aire valley, though Rombalds Moor north of the Aire is a continuation of the gritstone landscape and certainly merits inclusion here. Further south, the gritstone includes the Dark Peak areas of Kinder Scout, Bleaklow and Black Hill, which are featured in other books in the Freedom to Roam series: our convenient southern border for this volume is marked by the line of the M62 across Rishworth Moor.

As will quickly be discovered, stone plays a key role in the walks in this book. There are, first, the typical gritstone rocky outcrops to be visited – different walks will lead you to fine examples such as the Dove Stones near Boulsworth Hill, the Alcomden Stones near Stanbury and Great Edge at Widdop, all areas which it has only been possible to visit legally since the introduction of access legislation. From the Hitching Stone (Walk 3) and the Thimble Stones (Walk 2) in the north to Robin Hood's Bed and Blackstone Edge (Walk 12) in the south, a whole walking holiday could be planned around striking features of the Pennine landscape.

In addition, there are the natural rocks to be found on the moors which are of particular interest because of the role they have played in very early human history. Mention has already been made of the extraordinary prehistoric cup-and-rings and markings to be found carved on rocks and stones on Rombalds

Moor. Stones with prehistoric carvings are still regularly being discovered by those who look for them, and – outside Rombalds Moor and some other areas in north Yorkshire – little serious attempt has yet been made to systematically catalogue the extent of these carvings. This may be worth bearing in mind as you scrabble about, say, on the Great Saucer Stones (Walk 4) or Great Edge (Walk 7).

Other, slightly more recent, stones give the walks in this book extra interest. There are standing stoops (high stones to demarcate boundaries and to guide travellers) in the most unlikely moorland areas. There are Lanshaw Lad and Lanshaw Lass, for example, on Rombalds Moor (Walk 1). There is the medieval Aiggin Stone on Blackstone Edge (Walk 12). There is the Oxenhope Stoop (Walk 6), and the Two Lads (Walk 10), and lonely Churn Milk Joan, with its curious tradition that coins are left on the top of the stone by travellers who pass (Walk 9). There is the stone called Te Deum, carved with the Latin words *Te Deum Laudamus*, high up on the hillside between Withens Clough and the Calder valley (Walk 10).

And finally there are even more recent additions to the landscape, such as the carefully crafted stone known as Lad o' Crow Hill, with its fine serif letters (Walk 5), or the mysterious little stone set in the moors near Warley, which carries the enigmatic message 'A sinner saved by grace' (Walk 9). What are the stories behind these stones? We will probably never know.

So the desolate and wild moors of the south Pennines turn out on closer inspection not to be so empty of interest after all. There is much to discover here in the open country. There are, in short, so many excuses for taking time to go walking.

WALK 1

PREHISTORIC ILKLEY MOOR

DIFFICULTY 🥾 DISTANCE 5 miles (8 km)

| ILKLEY | ASHLAR CHAIR | LANSHAW LAD AND TWELVE APOSTLES | HAYSTACK ROCK | COW AND CALF | ILKLEY |

MAP OS Explorer 297, Lower Wharfedale and Washburn Valley

STARTING POINT Edge of Ilkley Moor, near White Wells (GR 116470)

PARKING In the White Wells car park, or in nearby roads

PUBLIC TRANSPORT Ilkley is well served by buses from neighbouring towns and by trains from Leeds and Bradford. Half-mile walk (0.8 km) to the walk start, or take local bus W3.

A journey back in time, to discover some of the extraordinary prehistoric remains on Ilkley Moor. Relatively easy walking

▶ Walk up to White Wells, the white-washed cottage on the moor overlooking the town ❶.

■ White Wells has an interesting history as a miniature spa and bath house, with its story going back to the middle of the eighteenth century.

Treatment for those hoping to be cured of a whole range of ailments, from arthritis to eye inflammations, consisted of the 'cold water cure' – in other words, being immersed in water straight out of the moor. Originally, the plunge pools (two were built) were

© Crown Copyright 10004293 2004

This map does not show all access land designated under the 2000 access legislation

open to the elements and only later was a roof provided as shelter. There is a small museum inside the building which tells the full story of White Wells.

One of the two plunge pools is still available for use today. There are mass dips organized at New Year and on other occasions during the year, but it is also possible to take the plunge at other times. Equip yourself with a towel and bathing wear, and report to the staff in the café next door. (By tradition, a flag is flown when the building is open.)

(Note: unusually detailed walk directions are given for parts of this walk, in order to help you find the carved stones that are mentioned in the text.)

▶ From White Wells, head south-east up the hill, following the right of way shown on the OS map as the Dales Way Link. The path climbs up, bearing left up stone steps to reach the top of Ilkley Crags. At the top, continue on the path until you arrive at a crossing of paths, beside a pile of stones. Turn left. When the path forks after a few hundred yards (metres), take the right-hand path as it drops down towards Backstone Beck. About 50 yards (50 m) from the bottom of the beck, turn right on to a path. After another 100 yards (100 m) or so, you will reach a flat stone right in the middle of

the track (GR 127462), carved with a series of fifty or more cups and rings ❷.

■ This is one of about 275 stones on Rombalds Moor (the name for the whole moor on which you are walking, including the moors directly above Ilkley) which have been found to have prehistoric carvings. Typical patterns are those of the cup (in other words a circular carved indention in the rock) or the cup-and-ring, where the indentation is surrounded by a ring. However, as this stone demonstrates, some of the stones combine these elements with other more elaborate patterns, including grooves and swirls.

Cup-and-ring stones have been discovered in other parts of the British Isles, and indeed in other parts of Europe, but the concentration of stones on Rombalds Moor is remarkable. The importance of this area began to become clear in Victorian times. The first written report was published in 1869, and archaeologists started to become seriously interested ten years later, when further studies were written. However it is only in very recent times that a concerted attempt has been made to systematically examine and record the full extent of the carved stones in the area, in a project which has been undertaken by local people, initially as an adult education class and subsequently working as the Ilkley Archaeology Group. Their enthusiasm and efforts have resulted in what is currently the definitive book on the subject, *Prehistoric Rock Art of the West Riding*, written by K.J.S. Boughey and E.A. Vickerman and published by the West Yorkshire Archaeology Service and English Heritage. The volume includes grid references, to ten figures, for each stone (this is perhaps one occasion when walkers may justifiably consider that GPS equipment has value).

These carvings are several thousand years old, but quite how many thousand years is an issue on which specialist opinion is divided. The Bronze Age is generally regarded as starting in Britain around 2000 BC, and some people have suggested that the carvings date from the middle Bronze Age period, which would make them up to 3500 years old. Others suggest that they were carved in the early Bronze Age, pushing the date back by up to 500 years, and there has also been discussion about whether they are earlier still, dating back to late neolithic times. Some carvings on Rombalds Moor, such as those on the Swastika Stone (see page 36), may be somewhat later.

Despite the efforts of the Ilkley Archaeology Society, as mentioned in the introduction it is unlikely that all the carved stones on the moor have yet been identified – so it is well worth paying attention to your surroundings as you walk.

▶ page 30

Lanshaw Lad

Prehistory on Rombalds Moor is not limited to the carved stones. Just across the valley of Backstone Beck at this point can be seen a walled enclosure, which was built in the later Bronze Age (roughly between 800 and 500 BC). Excavation of this enclosure demonstrated that the site had been used sporadically since about 2500 BC. Part of the walling has been reconstructed.

▶ Continue on the path, keeping the beck on your left.

■ The walled sheepfold to your right is relatively modern, not prehistoric. However there are a number of standing stones among the walling which are likely to date back to prehistoric times and may represent an old stone circle. Paul Bennett, who is interested in the mystical and ritual as well as the archaeological aspects of stones, describes in his book *The Old Stones of Elmet* a psychic experience with ghostly figures which he and a friend went through one summer night at this location.

▶ The path rejoins the main Dales Way Link route across the moor. Turn left. A stone marker, the Lanshaw Lad, comes into sight on the hill brow ahead.

The suggested route branches off right shortly after a stretch of boardwalk, to take in a visit to the Ashlar Chair ❸.

■ The Ashlar Chair can be found on the boundary between Ilkley and Keighley parishes, at the point on the moor where stone walls meet. This much-eroded gritstone rock was reported 100 years ago as having carved cups and grooves, but these are no longer visible and this is not a stone with much to interest archaeologists today.

The Ashlar Chair does, however, attract visitors interested in mysticism and paganism, for whom the rock has important powers and significance.

▶ From here, make for Lanshaw Lad ❹. A well-walked path can be found, heading across the top of the moor.

■ The Lanshaw Lad is a boundary stone, perhaps of Anglo-Saxon origin, which also acts as a stoop to help travellers find their path across the moor.

Just beyond is the stone circle known as the Twelve Apostles ❺. This stone circle is presumed to date back to prehistoric times, though the stones themselves are likely to have been moved and rearranged over the years. Like the Ashlar Chair, the Twelve Apostles is also an important site of pilgrimage for those interested in mysticism and old religions, and it is the focus of a mid-summer solstice gathering.

▶ Having visited Lanshaw Lad, you would be remiss not to visit Lanshaw Lass, another early boundary stone. Head north-east over the open moor, across the wet ground above High Lanshaw Dam. The Lanshaw Lass is lying on its side; the site is marked with a large, modern, yellow boundary marker ❻.

From Lanshaw Lass, a good path can be picked up running initially north-east to Green Crag and then north-west. The path heads straight past a large triangular stone known as the Idol Rock (GR 133459), whose carvings are modern, and then to a small flat rock, the Idol Stone (GR 133459) ❼.

■ This unmistakable low stone is carved with a series of linear cups and grooves, to create a waffle-like design.

▶ The path continues, towards a large rock which resembles an old-fashioned haystack. This is indeed known as the Haystack Rock (GR 130463) ❽.

■ The Haystack Rock has about seventy cups, ten with rings, as well as several interlinking carved grooves.

Close at hand are two other well-known carved stones that may be worth a short diversion. The Pancake Rock (GR 134462) is balanced dramatically on the edge of a ridge of rocks. The flat surface of the rock is eroded, but a number of cups and grooves can be seen. The Planets Rock, with a fascinating pattern which some associate with the planets in the solar system, is also close by (GR 130464).

▶ Take one of the paths heading down the hillside from the Haystack Rock to the Cow and Calf rock outcrops below ❾.

■ After so much discussion of prehistoric rock carvings, mention should perhaps be made of the astonishing number of nineteenth-century carvings on the Cow and Calf rocks, which spread out to cover all available surfaces. The Cow and Calf rocks remain a honeypot for summer visitors.

▶ Close at hand, however, is one final prehistoric carved rock to visit, perhaps the most famous of all: the Hangingstones Quarry rock. From the most westerly of the

Cow and Calf rocks, drop down into the large Hangingstones Quarry, one of the main sources of building stone for the town of Ilkley, and then climb up to the rocky promontory on the right-hand (north) side of the quarry.

■ This rock has a particularly unusual series of carvings, including many curved symbol-like designs. It was saved from being destroyed by quarrying in the nineteenth century only after the intervention of a visitor.

The Hangingstones rock has also been given a contemporary Celtic knot, carved in 1994. More worryingly, modern graffiti is beginning to appear near the prehistoric carvings. There is, perhaps, an argument for protecting this stone behind railings, as has been done for the Swastika Stone (see page 36).

▶ From the Hangingstones rock, find one of the several paths through the bracken and heather to White Wells.

WALK 2

ON ROMBALDS MOOR

DIFFICULTY 👟 👟 **DISTANCE** 7½ miles (12 km)

ILKLEY — SWASTIKA STONE — BUCK STONES — THIMBLE STONES — BADGER STONE — ILKLEY

MAP OS Explorer 297, Lower Wharfedale and Washburn Valley

STARTING POINT As Walk 1: edge of Ilkley Moor, near White Wells (GR 116470)

PARKING In the White Wells car park, or in nearby roads

PUBLIC TRANSPORT Ilkley is well served with buses from neighbouring towns and by trains from Leeds and Bradford. Half-mile walk (0.8 km) to the walk start, or take local bus W3.

Another opportunity to enjoy Rombalds Moor and to visit some of the prehistoric carved stones to be found there.

▶ This walk begins easily, following a popular route on Ilkley Moor. Take one of the footpaths close to the moor edge, heading west past the little

reservoir near Heber's Ghyll to the Swastika Stone ❶.

■ The Swastika Stone is one of the most famous of the carved stones on Rombalds Moor. The stone carving – a swirling design, with four arms, one of which has an extra tail – was first discovered in the mid-nineteenth century, when

33

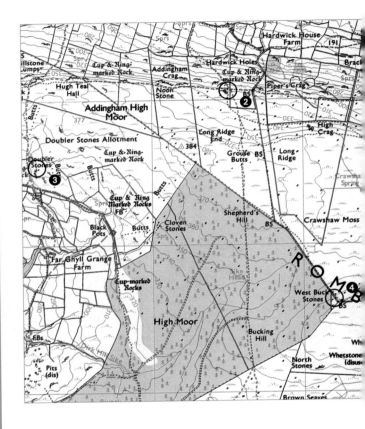

moss and vegetation were cleared from the stone, and was first publicized in an article in the *Leeds Mercury* in 1871. The unique design on this stone has fascinated archaeologists ever since,

and has also attracted considerable attention from those with a more mystical approach to Ilkley's prehistoric carved stones.

The swastika symbol has been found elsewhere in

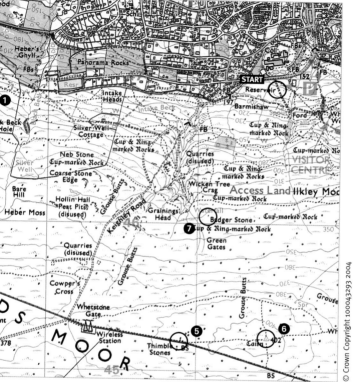

This map does not show all access land designated under the 2000 access legislation

Europe dating back to very early times, for example on pottery and ornaments found in Troy and Mycenae, and also elsewhere in the world. The broken-cross design is a traditional Hindu symbol, for instance (this symbol is the reverse of the swastika used by the German Nazis, incidentally). However the Ilkley symbol, with its curved rather than straight arms, is rather different from the

Hindu design. The Ilkley pattern has been found on a rock in Italy, and on a small number of rocks in Sweden.

Because the design is so different from the usual cup-and-ring designs elsewhere on Rombalds Moor, experts have recently suggested that it may have been carved later, during the Iron Age rather than the early Bronze Age. Nevertheless, this stone is still a fascinating prehistoric object.

The Swastika Stone is now protected from vandalism behind railings. In front of the carving itself, which can initially be hard to make out, is a larger, modern copy of the design.

▶ Continue along the well-walked path, enjoying the exceptionally fine views over the Wharfe valley and beyond to the Yorkshire Dales.

■ If the Swastika Stone has stimulated your interest in the prehistory of Rombalds Moor, there are several other carved stones which can be found just off the path. One, a few yards (metres) west of the Swastika Stone and a few yards (metres) to your left is an old gatepost now lying flat; this has two cup marks, at least one of which also has a surrounding ring. Another, a little further on (GR 090470), is the Sepulchre Stone, with a number of worn cups and grooves. Further on again is the flat rock known as Piper's Crag Stone (GR 084471) ❷ which has over thirty carved cups, in a series of rings and grooves.

▶ At this point, it's possible to turn south along the wall edge across Long Ridge End. It's tempting, however, to continue across Addingham High Moor to reach Black Hill, and then turn south to look for the Doubler Stones ❸.

■ The Doubler Stones are a pair of highly dramatic eroded rocks, one in particular remarkably resembling a mushroom. They have been caused by the erosion of softer sandstone pillars, leaving behind harder gritstone. Both stones have carved cups.

▶ From the Doubler Stones, it is possible to cut across open moorland to the trig point marked on OS maps and from there to follow the edge of the forested area. This direct route currently involves crossing two stone walls, however. Great care should be taken not to displace stones, and some people will prefer to retrace their steps to avoid the risk.

Follow the wood edge in a south-easterly direction, keeping to the moor side of the wall. You will shortly reach the West and East Buck Stones ❹. These are large natural outcrops of rocks, none of which appears to have received prehistoric attention. Continue on the path to the communications station and then to the Thimble Stones ❺.

■ Although the Thimble Stones have impressive grooves and channels, these are generally considered to have been created by natural

forces rather than by human endeavour.

▶ From the Thimble Stones, turn towards the trig point almost due east ❻. The distant golf-ball shaped radomes of the US communications interception station at Menwith Hill can be seen in the distance to the north.

The next target is the Badger Stone (GR 110460 – it is worth using the grid reference, since the OS maps are not as clear as they might be about the stone's location). While it's possible to take a direct compass bearing and head across open moorland, most people will probably opt for the easier route and take the path which runs off northwards from the trig point. Turn left off this path after about ½ mile (0.8 km) to find the Badger Stone ❼, a large rock several feet (at least a metre) in height. Conveniently, a wooden seat has been placed next to the stone.

■ Another famous carved stone, the Badger Stone has a large number of cups and grooves carved into its south-facing side, and several cups

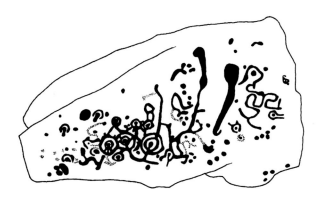

Carvings on the Badger Stone

and rings on the east side, suggesting half a swastika. Sadly, many of the carvings are now eroded, and the stone has also suffered from vandalism.

Near by, especially to the north and the east, there are several other smaller stones with carvings which can be tracked down.

▶ From the Badger Stone a footpath (not shown on maps) heads off through bracken in a north and north-easterly direction, to emerge directly above the White Wells car park.

That song – On Ilkla Moor baht 'at

There are not many songs as well known as *that* song about Ilkley Moor. There are also not many songs where the singers – particularly those from outside Yorkshire – frequently aren't too sure what they're singing about. (What precisely is the 'bar tat', for example?)

It is perhaps not surprising, therefore, if (even when alcohol is not involved) the quality of the singing leaves something to be desired. Yorkshire dialect specialist Arnold Kellett points out in his book *Basic Broad Yorkshire* some of the pitfalls: 'Well-known though the song is, it is often sung very badly, even by Yorkshire people, with the original West Riding dialect giving way to standard English vowels and vocabulary – Ilkley being pronounced "Ilkli" or "Ilklay" instead of *Ilkla*, "more" instead of *mooar*, "et" instead of *at*, "death of cold" instead of *deeath o' cowd* etc.'

Arnold Kellett, who worked as a modern languages teacher at a school in north Yorkshire, goes on to claim that 'Yorkshire dialect is virtually a foreign language in its spoken form, as far as speakers of standard English are concerned.' For southerners or others who are approaching Yorkshire as a second language, therefore, it may be worth providing a little translation. The song's correct title is spelled something like 'On Ilkla Mooar baht 'at', and it tells the sad tale of an unnamed man who catches his death of cold (or rather 'deeath o' cowd') by going courting on the moors without a hat. 'Baht', in other words, means 'without'. Initial 'h's are silent in Yorkshire dialect, as indeed they were in almost all English dialects outside East Anglia and Northumbria. (RP is the exception in this respect, rather than the norm.)

The song's original first line 'Wheer wor ta bahn when ah saw thee' may also cause some problems, 'bahn' meaning 'going'. 'Ta' is, of course, the familiar form of the second person, in conventional (if antique) standard English 'thou' but pronounced 'tha' or 'ta' in the West Riding where it is still used by some speakers today. The alternative first line, 'Wheeare 'es ta bin sin' ah saw thee?', although more widely sung nowadays, is generally regarded as less historically authentic.

So what, anyway, is the history of the song? Arnold Kellett is once again the person to turn to for help, as the author of the book called *On Ilkla Mooar Baht 'At*. There is no doubt about the tune: it was called Cranbrook and was composed very early in the nineteenth century as a hymn tune by a Methodist composer and boot- and shoe-maker from Kent called Thomas Clark. At that time it was a popular tune, used as the setting for a number of well-known Methodist hymns.

The words of 'Ilkla Moor' began life therefore as something of a parody to this established hymn tune, almost certainly some time in the middle of the nineteenth century. The first time 'Ilkla Moor' found itself in print was in 1916, but as Arnold Kellett points out by this stage the song was already well established locally among singers. Kellett's theory is that the song may well have been composed during a chapel choir outing to Ilkley, and he suggests that the choir in question may have come from the Halifax area. Another story suggests that a choir from Heptonstall near Hebden Bridge – just up the Calder valley from Halifax – may have been the culprit.

For non-natives who want the real thing, and are prepared to work on their glottal stops and vowel sounds, the words of the song are available from Ilkley tourist office in a leaflet published by the council. Arnold Kellett's own preferred version has a few minor spelling changes from the council's version, which he says are designed to better reflect dialect pronunciation. Without the innumerable repeats, this version goes as follows:

Wheeare wo' ta bahn when Ah saw thee
On Ilkla Mooar baht 'at?

Tha's bin a-coortin' Mary Jane
On Ilkla Mooar baht 'at.

Tha's bahn ter get thi deeath o' cowd
On Ilkla Mooar baht 'at.

Then wi s'll 'a' ter bury thee
On Ilkla Mooar baht 'at.

Then t'wurrums 'll come an' eyt thee up
On Ilkla Mooar baht 'at.

Then t'ducks 'll come an' eyt up t'wurrums
On Ilkla Mooar baht 'at.

Then wi s'll come an' eyt up t'ducks
On Ilkla Mooar baht 'at.

Then wi s'll all 'ave etten thee
On Ilkla Mooar baht 'at.

That's wheeare wi get us ooan back!
On Ilkla Mooar baht 'at.

WALK 3

THE HITCHING STONE

DIFFICULTY 🥾 🥾 🥾 🥾 **DISTANCE 7½ miles (12 km)**

| COWLING | ICKORNSHAW MOOR | WOLF STONES | HITCHING STONE | WAINMAN'S PINNACLE | COWLING |

MAP OS Explorer OL21, South Pennines

STARTING POINT Cowling village (GR 973431)

PARKING In Cowling village

PUBLIC TRANSPORT Regular buses between Colne/Burnley and Keighley

A walk out and back across Ickornshaw Moor, one of the wilder stretches of moorland in the south Pennines. Relatively easy walking out, followed by 3 miles (4.8 km) of much tougher walking across rough open country.

▶ From the centre of Cowling, make for the Pennine Way running south. Either simply walk along the main road heading west, or use one of the footpaths to join the route just south of the village.

Follow the Pennine Way as it skirts Dean Brow Beck, and heads south on to the open moors ❶.

■ This stretch of the Pennine Way gets a poor review from Wainwright, in his *Pennine Way Companion*: 'an arduous little wilderness', he claims, summarizing the overall

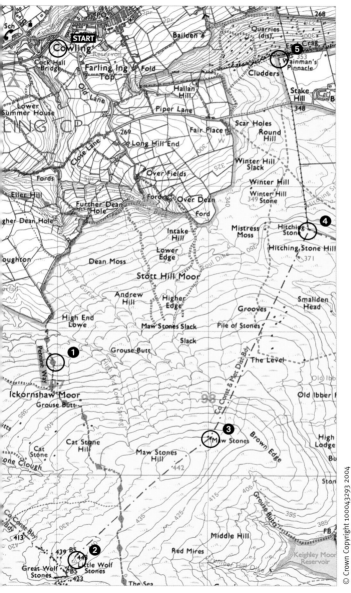

START

Cowling

5

4

3

1

2

experience as 'mediocre stuff'. However, compared with some of the earlier stretches of peat moorland faced by Pennine Way walkers – earlier, that is, for those people following the usual south–north route – Ickornshaw Moor is relatively kind. Certainly, the paving work which has been carried out since Wainwright's time helps to get walkers over the wettest areas of the moor.

▶ Continue on the Pennine Way until the brow of the hill is reached, and the Worth valley comes into sight ahead. At this point, turn off the Pennine Way and head south-westwards to the trig point a little way off, at the Wolf Stones ❷. A trod (faint path) will lead you there.

■ Somewhat unexpectedly, the Wolf Stones trig point offers an excellent panoramic view – Pendle Hill and Boulsworth close at hand in one direction, the Yorkshire Dales (including Penyghent, Ingleborough and Great Whernside) in the other.

▶ Retrace your steps from the Wolf Stones, and this time cross over the Pennine Way, keeping in the same north-easterly direction. Another faint trod will bring you to the Maw Stones ❸.

Near the Maw Stones the trod disappears, and there is no option but to head off across the open moor. This next section is pathless, but the line to follow roughly corresponds to the West Yorkshire/North Yorkshire boundary shown on the map. Provided there is visibility, there is in fact no problem in navigation: the Hitching Stone can be clearly seen ahead, while behind it, in almost a straight line, is Lund's Tower on Earl Crag. In poor visibility, a compass bearing is needed.

Continue across the moor until you reach the Hitching Stone ❹.

■ Of all the rocks, standing stones and gritstone outcrops featured in this book – and there is certainly no shortage of them – the Hitching Stone is surely the most dramatic. This great cube of rock is the size of a small house. It has been suggested that the rock may have originated in the Earl Crag outcrop, just to the north, and been carried to its present position by a glacier during the Ice Age.

The Hitching Stone today is at the boundaries of three parishes, and in past times it may also have been used to set boundaries. John Thornhill, writing in 1989 in the journal *Bradford Antiquary* states that the historical wapentakes of Skyrack and Staincliffe met here ('wapentake' is the Yorkshire term for what elsewhere were known as hundreds). Discussing Anglo-Saxon and Danish gatherings, he asks, 'Could this impressive flat-topped stone, a conspicuous object on a featureless moor, have been a meeting-place of the local Moot or Thing?' Until relatively recent times, the festival of Lammas (1 August) was commemorated at the Hitching Stone with a local fair for the people of the Cowling and Sutton parishes. Accounts tell of horse races being held across the moorland during the fair celebrations.

If you choose to scramble up the south-facing side of the Hitching Stone, you will find a surprise at the top: not the rock shelf which might be expected but a deep rock pool, full of rainwater. The western face also is interesting, since high up is a natural opening in the rock which has been called by some the Priest's Chair or the Druid's Chair. Running down diagonally through the rock, passing the Priest's Chair, is a circular shaft or flue, which once again is a natural phenomenon. The explanation is that this was caused by the effect of time and weather on a fossilized tree which once was embedded in the rock.

However, there is also another explanation for the shaft, as recorded in folklore: that the stone was magically flung to its present location by a witch who 'hitched' it up using a broomstick – and that the hole remains to show where the broomstick had been inserted.

▶ page 48

Wainman's Pinnacle

For those so inclined, the Hitching Stone can be visited for its mystical powers. Paul Bennett in *The Old Stones of Elmet* calls on his readers to 'feel the spirit nature of this, one of Elmet's most powerful stones' (Elmet was the old Celtic kingdom in what is now roughly the area of West Yorkshire). He states, 'Its geomantic virtues represent the forces of life, death, rebirth and Illumination.'

Whatever your reasons for making the visit, the Hitching Stone is certainly memorable.

▶ From here, follow a path beside the moorside wall north to Buck Stone Lane. Cross over, to climb up to the base of Wainman's Pinnacle ❺.

■ As Wainwright put it, 'gentlemen of the West Riding had a liking for erecting monuments on the hilltops around their homes'. Earl Crag offers the choice of two.

Wainman's Pinnacle and Lund's Tower carry the family names of local gentry who lived in the area for several generations. Wainman's Pinnacle (also known as Cowling Pinnacle) is believed to have been erected some time after 1815 – perhaps, like Stoodley Pike (see pages 114–15) to commemorate the end of the Napoleonic Wars. It was damaged by lightning and was rebuilt in 1900.

Lund's Tower was built later in the nineteenth century and is rather more interesting, since it is possible to climb up inside to reach the 'battlements'. Take care not to bang your head at the top of the steps.

▶ From the follies at Earl Crag, return to the starting point of this walk in Cowling village.

WALK 4

GREAT SAUCER STONES

DIFFICULTY 👢 👢 **DISTANCE 8 miles (13 km)**

WYCOLLER   GREAT SAUCER STONES   BOULSWORTH HILL   WYCOLLER

MAP OS Explorer OL21, South Pennines

STARTING POINT Wycoller Country Park

PARKING Car park for Wycoller Country Park (GR 927394), or upper car park on the Colne–Stanbury road (GR 935393)

PUBLIC TRANSPORT Regular buses run from Burnley, Nelson and Colne to Trawden (1½ miles/2.5 km); or adapt the walk to start from Trawden.

An approach to Boulsworth Hill from the north. Option of some rough moorland walking.

▶ This walk begins at Wycoller, the attractive hamlet near Trawden which is now run as a conservation area and country park by Lancashire County Council.

■ Wycoller is a deservedly popular destination for weekend visitors. Part of its charm is the way in which little Wycoller Beck runs through the settlement. The stream is crossed by a series of bridges, including a twin-arched packhorse bridge which dates back to medieval times, and a clapper bridge, which is made of stone slabs supported on stone piers. The earliest bridge, however, is to be found a little

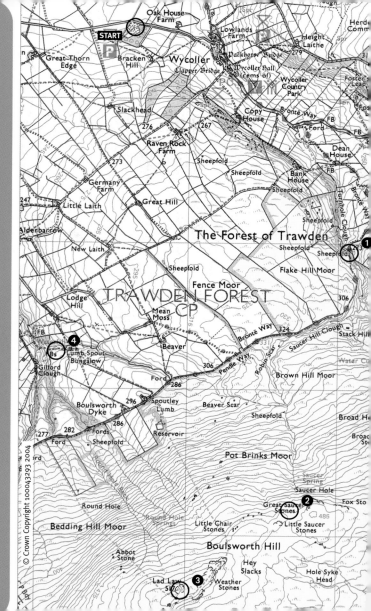

© Crown Copyright 100043293 2004

upstream: this clam bridge is a single slab of gritstone which was carefully laid between the two banks. It is thought to be at least a thousand years old, and is a scheduled ancient monument. The clam bridge was damaged by flash floods in 1989 and again in 1990, and was restored in 1991.

Wycoller has its own Bronte connection: Charlotte Bronte is believed by some to have based Ferndean Manor in *Jane Eyre* on Wycoller Hall. The Hall, which is now in ruins, was built at the end of the sixteenth century by a local family called the Hartleys, and was ill-advisedly extended in the late eighteenth century by a distant descendant, Henry Cunliffe. When he died in 1818 he was heavily indebted and Wycoller Hall remained empty thereafter; it would therefore have been unoccupied at the time of Charlotte Bronte. Stone from the Hall was removed and re-used elsewhere in the neighbourhood.

Like the Hall, the village itself slowly decayed. After the Second World War, a Friends of Wycoller group was established which attempted to revive the community and tidy up the remains of the Hall. Wycoller and the surrounding land was finally acquired by the county council in 1973.

The county council has created a small exhibition and information centre in the Barn, a fine aisled building constructed in the 1630s which is worth visiting. Wycoller also offers a privately run café and gift shop.

▶ Walk through Wycoller and up the tarmac track beside the beck. There are various routes from here to the open moors, but perhaps the shortest is to take the concessionary footpath up the side of Turnhole Clough, shortly after passing the clam bridge. (This footpath leaves just beside the farm track to Dean House, as the Bronte Way to Haworth turns left.) Follow the footpath through pleasant woods until you reach the moorland.

▶ page 54

Near Brink Ends, the path joins a long-established bridleway along the base of the Boulsworth flank ❶. This track is now the route of both the Pendle Way (the small 'witch' signposts point the way) and the Bronte Way.

The track turns south-west beside Stack Hill Clough. Here you can pick your own route uphill across the open moors. An easier alternative to tussock-hopping is to continue on the bridleway for a few hundred yards (metres), and then to follow the clough which heads due south to the Saucer Hole. If you are lucky, you will find a footpath used by shooters to reach grouse butts.

■ The Great Saucer Stones are well worth exploring ❷. There are persistent local stories of a rocky cave hereabouts, with animal carvings. This sounds exciting, but be warned that the carvings are thought to be of relatively modern origin and the cave itself is extremely difficult to track down.

▶ At the Saucer Stones, a path runs along the brow of Boulsworth Hill, past further outcrops of rock up to the trig point at the summit itself (see pages 56–9) ❸.

From Boulsworth, there is an easy descent using the concessionary footpath created several years ago by North West Water (now United Utilities). For more ambitious walking, one option would be to make a diversion south to visit the Dove Stones (see pages 82–3). Another possibility is to continue south-westwards, heading towards Black Clough. This is very heavy going across rough ground. The target here is likely to be the romantic-sounding Robin Hood's House shown on the map. Unfortunately, the reality is rather less romantic: the walls of a ruined building, set beside the clough.

■ Before you reach Black Clough, it's possible to find an old boundary stone, marked with the number 8, the letters TF and with what could be the letters TP. TF stands for Trawden Forest, the parish to the east of the boundary stone. The parish name recalls the fact that in medieval times the land from Trawden to Boulsworth was a hunting ground ('forest' in its older usage meant royal hunting lands; this is the usage which has given us both the Forest of Bowland and the New Forest).

▶ Whichever route you choose from Boulsworth, make your way down the hillside to rejoin the Pendle Way/Bronte Way bridleway. It's possible to follow this track back, along the moor edge, all the way to Wycoller. A pleasant alternative is to take the field footpath behind Boulsworth Dyke farmhouse which heads off north-westwards, or the similar path which leaves just beyond Spoutley Lumb. Both paths will take you, in less than ½ mile (0.8 km), to the waterfall of Lumb Spout ❹.

■ Lumb Spout was a popular beauty spot in Victorian times, when a café was established to service visitors' needs.
Today Lumb Spout is much less frequently visited. The waterfall itself may not be particularly impressive, but its setting, in an old woodland glade, is pleasant and unexpected.

▶ From Lumb Spout, it's easy to return to Wycoller using field footpaths. One obvious route passes Lodge Hill house, heading towards Bank House. Beyond here you can pick up the footpath along Turnhole Clough again, for the final mile (1.6 km) or so into Wycoller.

The view from Boulsworth Hill

Boulsworth keeps a low profile. Unlike neighbouring Pendle Hill, just across the valley beyond Burnley and Nelson, this is a hill which doesn't attract large crowds. Its name doesn't sell guidebooks and even enthusiastic hill walkers may struggle to locate it on the map. Boulsworth? – no, sorry, don't know it.

It could have been very different. If Tom Stephenson, the man whose vision led to the creation of the Pennine Way, had had his way, walkers on Britain's first and best-known national trail would have walked up through the rough moorland grasses above Widdop to arrive on the summit of Boulsworth – and would have experienced the moment when, suddenly, the view opens out, north to the Yorkshire Dales and the Three Peaks, west beyond Pendle to the Forest of Bowland, and east towards the plain of York and perhaps, far away, the start of the North Yorks Moors.

The dream of the Pennine Way was first set out by Stephenson in a famous newspaper article in the *Daily Herald* entitled 'Wanted – a Long Green Trail'. Stephenson was inspired by the examples from North America of the Appalachian Trail, running for 2000 miles (3220 km) from Maine to Georgia, and the John Muir Trail in California. But he was angry that access prohibitions had prevented the creation of a similar long-distance trail in Britain. 'When two American girls wrote asking advice about a tramping holiday in England, I wondered what they would think of our island, particularly of the restrictions placed in the way of those who wished to see some of our most captivating scenery,' he wrote.

His solution was to be 'a Pennine Way from the Peak to the Cheviots'. Stephenson went on to imagine 'carefree youngsters' following his trail, passing through the Peak District to Bleaklow and the Saddleworth Moors before arriving at Blackstone Edge. 'Then, steering between the industrial blackspots, on beyond the vale of Cliviger, they would stand on Boulsworth, and behold, on the one hand, the level brow of Pendle . . . and on the other the dark moors which inspired the Brontes,' he wrote.

Stephenson was writing in 1935. It took many years, including the social upheavals of the war and the passing in 1949 of the landmark National Parks and Access to the Countryside Act, before the Pennine Way became a reality. Indeed, the Pennine

Pendle Hill, as seen from Boulsworth Hill

Way was only designated Britain's first official long-distance walking route in 1965.

In one respect, however, Stephenson's vision was not realized. The route for the Pennine Way as it approaches those 'dark moors which inspired the Brontes' does not include the summit of Boulsworth. Instead the path is routed a little way to the east, past the Walshaw reservoirs – a fine stretch of heather moorland, but one which lacks the vistas which would otherwise have been available.

It was the landowners' reluctance to open up their lands which kept the Pennine Way walkers away from the Boulsworth plateau. In fact, until the passing of the 2000 access legislation, the Countryside and Rights of Way Act, there was no official right of way on to the hillside. North West Water had helpfully created two concessionary footpaths from the Lancashire side to the top of Boulsworth, but walkers from Yorkshire had no direct access at all. The options were either to make a long detour or to risk a gamekeeper's wrath by trespassing. Perhaps it is not surprising that Boulsworth Hill isn't better known.

Pre-metric maps gave the height of Boulsworth Hill as 1699 ft. Today's maps declare it is 517 m high. Either way – leaving aside Pendle Hill, which stands a little apart – this makes it the highest ground in the main Pennine chain between the Yorkshire Dales and the Peak District.

As has been mentioned, on good days there are views to match the height. In fact, it is quite possible to see Blackpool Tower from Boulsworth, even though it is more than forty miles (sixty-five kilometres) away to the west. The tower looks like a tiny stick, rising up from the flat ground which is framed on the left by the west Pennine hills and on the right by Pendle. When the sun is low and is shining directly on the tower, the sight is unmistakable.

Some people have claimed to see more than just Blackpool Tower from Boulsworth. The early twentieth-century writer

Whiteley Turner in his book *A Spring-Time Saunter Round and About Bronte Land* quotes an earlier writer as follows:

> The late F.A. Leyland, in a contribution to the *Halifax Courier* years ago, wrote of standing on Boulsworth one 9th of June, when the mist and rains of the forenoon had suddenly cleared away, and before the sun had had time to raise vapour. Through his telescope he stated he saw the houses on the beach at Blackpool; the steeple of the Catholic Church in Talbot Road, and the wind-mills in the neighbourhood; the Horse-Bank at Lytham, objects at Southport, and the sand that lie between there and the sea; of watching the shrimping boats and fishing-smacks, and observing a large steamer passing . . .

Incidentally, problems of access to Boulsworth are nothing new. Whiteley Turner, who had a shrewd idea that he was trespassing to reach the summit, recalled a court case in 1885 when three pillars of the Halifax community had been summonsed to court to explain their presence on the hill.

It is not surprising that when a campaign was launched in the south Pennines area in the mid-1990s calling for open access to the local moors the focus was particularly on this one hill. Access to Boulsworth Campaign (ABC) engaged in a spirited series of rallies and meetings to publicize its cause, bringing both television cameras and senior politicians up to the moors around Boulsworth to see for themselves.

A word on pronunciation: Boulsworth is now increasingly pronounced with the first syllable rhyming with 'rolls'. Some local people, however, continue with an older pronunciation, rhyming the first part of the word with 'rules'.

WALK 5

THE LAD O' CROW HILL

DIFFICULTY 👢 👢 👢 **DISTANCE** 5½ miles (9 km)

PONDEN — PONDEN KIRK — ALCOMDEN — CROW HILL — LAD O' CROW HILL — PONDEN

MAP OS Explorer OL21, South Pennines

STARTING POINT Beside Ponden reservoir (GR 994370)

PARKING Cross the Ponden reservoir dam (following signs to Ponden House), turn right and park beside the reservoir.

PUBLIC TRANSPORT Hourly buses (no Sunday service) as well as a more infrequent local bus service (including Sundays) from Keighley and Haworth to Stanbury (1 mile/1.6 km from Ponden). Recently, a special service has run on summer Sundays only from Haworth station to Ponden Mill. Check locally.

This walk visits the heart of the so-called 'Bronte Moors', including both the impressive outcrop of rocks known as the Alcomden Stones and Crow Hill. Rough moorland walking between Alcomden Stones and Crow Hill.

▶ From the south-west corner of Ponden reservoir take the footpath up the track to Lower Slack farmhouse. At the house, find the footpath immediately to the right of the main building, to walk beside a stone wall. Follow this path on the level through two fields, and then turn half-left up the right-hand side of a wall, heading up the hill towards a distant finger-post. Once here, turn right to Ponden Clough.

Follow the right of way high above Ponden Clough, enjoying the views across to the other side. Shortly the path arrives at a smaller, deep-cut valley, Middle Moor Clough. It is worth continuing straight ahead here for a short distance, to arrive at the large, almost perpendicular rock known as Ponden Kirk ❶.

■ The strange name Ponden Kirk might suggest a religious association. In fact, the legends linked to the rock suggest, if anything, a pre-Christian significance. Some writers have attempted to claim that the rock may have had druidical connections.

The natural cleft in the rock has certainly attracted attention over the years. Whiteley Turner, a Halifax writer working in the early years of the twentieth century, reported that 'According to tradition, maidens (some say bachelors, too) who successfully creep through the aperture will be married within the year.'

To inspect the cleft at close quarters – or to attempt this feat yourself – it's necessary to take some care in scrambling down the hillside from the top of the rock.

▶ Retrace your steps from Ponden Kirk to the edge of Middle Moor Clough. Now turn right off the right of way, up the clough. The trod heading up the right-hand side of the clough will probably provide the easiest walking. Halfway up, you may need to make a small diversion to avoid wet ground.

■ The map here gives the name Robin Hood's Well to the spring just to the west of Middle Moor Clough, one of a number of references to Robin Hood to be found in the Yorkshire moors. Yorkshire claims Robin Hood as one of its own, alleging that Nottinghamshire's case is historically much weaker (see pages 108–9).

▶ At the top of Middle Moor Clough, the first of the Alcomden Stones come into sight ❷.

■ Almost everyone walking this way will want to pause and explore the Alcomden Stones. This outcrop (publicly accessible only since the introduction of access legislation) enjoys great views – always providing, of course, that the weather is good.

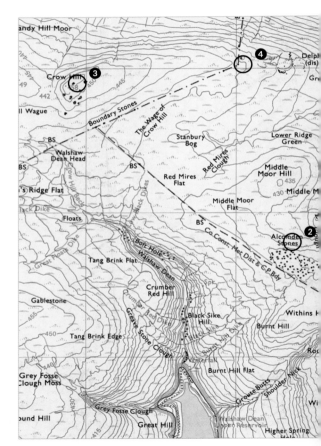

The stones are scattered across the hillside, in and among the heather and bracken, but your eye is likely to focus on the centrepiece of the Alcomden Stones, the flat rock which rests horizontally on two other rocks. In Victorian times, it was suggested that this could

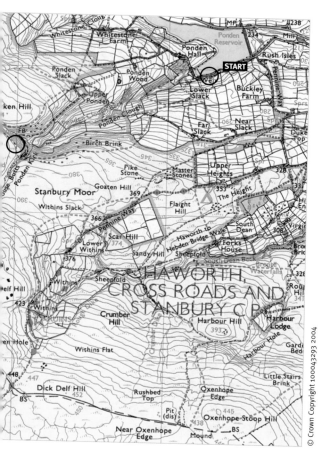

© Crown Copyright 1000043293 2004

represent a prehistoric dolmen-type edifice (with, of course, the inevitable association with druids). It is not necessary to accept this theory, however, to enjoy a visit here.

▶ From the Alcomden Stones, make for Crow Hill, 1 mile (1.6 km) or so away to the north-west. This is very rough country, and the direct route to Crow Hill involves skirting Stanbury Bog, the site of the 1824 'bog burst' (see pages 67–8). A better route may be to continue down the hillside from the stones, looking out for a small drainage ditch which runs from north-west to south-east. Turn right here. Initially, there is hardly even a faint trod to follow but gradually a better-defined path emerges, running just to the left of the ditch. If you have successfully found this route you will shortly come across a boundary stone marked KC 1902. (The stone, originally erected by Keighley Corporation, marks the current boundary between Calderdale and Bradford.)

Keep to the trod beside the ditch, through at least two boggy areas, aiming straight for Crow Hill. You will pass another KC 1902 stone before eventually you find yourself climbing up the gentle slope of Crow Hill ❸.

■ 'The wind on Crow Hill was her darling,' says Ted Hughes in a poem dedicated to Emily Bronte. Hughes may be using poetic licence, but certainly Emily Bronte did explore the moors close to her home in Haworth. Charlotte Bronte wrote after her death, 'My sister loved the moors. Flowers brighter than the rose bloomed in the blackest of the heath for her; out of a sullen hollow in a livid hillside her mind could make an Eden.' Emily Bronte herself once wrote:

I dream of moor and misty hill
Where evening closes dark and still.

Crow Hill can certainly be misty, but walkers will hope to find it in sunnier mood, if only to enjoy the fine views north, towards the Yorkshire

Dales, and west to nearby Pendle Hill.

▶ From the top of Crow Hill turn towards the east, keeping on the brow of the hill as it begins gently to slope downhill. (Avoid dropping down to the north of Crow Hill, towards Watersheddles reservoir.) With luck, you will find a trod to assist you through the tussocks.

As the hillside slowly drops towards an old delph (quarry),

look out for a triangular stone poking out above the vegetation. This is the Lad o' Crow Hill ❹.

■ As well as the now familiar KC 1902 inscription, the Lad o' Crow Hill carries a much more intriguing inscription, in carefully carved lettering:

LAD
ORSCARR
ON CROW
HILL

Ponden reservoir

Not surprisingly, the stone has been subject to much discussion over the years, going back at least to the nineteenth century. The story told by Yorkshire writer Halliwell Sutcliffe is that the stone commemorates a boy caught on the moors in a snowstorm, who died close to the spot where it is now erected. The body was found on the boundary between two parishes, one in Lancashire and one in Yorkshire, neither of which was prepared to meet the expenses of burying the corpse – and so eventually he was buried where he was found.

It is unfortunately true that people can succumb on the moors in rough winter weather. However in this case the story of the Lad of Crow Hill seems unlikely to be more than historical fiction. The word 'lad' has long been used in this part of the north of England to mean a guide stone, the root coming from the same verb as 'lead'.

Orscarr is somewhat less easy to explain (unless you are prepared to accept that the unfortunate young man was named Oscar). One explanation is that 'scar' can mean a rocky outcrop or cliff in dialect use.

▶ From the Lad head down into the quarry, to pick up the shooting track. This final section of the walk is very easy, as the track descends gradually down to Ponden.

■ Just before reaching the starting point of the walk, you pass the attractive Ponden Hall on the left. This house was lived in for many generations by the Heaton family, as the stone inscription above the front door records: 'The Old House now standing was built by Robert Heaton for his son Michael Anno Domini 1634'.

Ponden Hall is generally held to be the model for Thrushcross Grange in *Wuthering Heights*.

The Stanbury Bog explosion

Stanbury Bog is not the best place to find yourself when the weather turns nasty. The desolate moorland between Crow Hill and the Alcomden Stones is drained by a series of streams which eventually find their way to the River Worth, but the ground remains resolutely wet, a damp and squelchy experience even during very dry weather.

Unlikely as it may seem, Stanbury Bog has had its moment in history. At about 6pm on the evening of 2 September 1824, something happened up here on the moor which caused the bog to erupt, and to send a spate of mud, water and rocks down the hillside towards Ponden and Stanbury. This was the event which came to be known as the Crow Hill Bog Burst, or the Crow Hill Earthquake, or simply the Phenomenon.

The event was reported in the *Leeds Mercury*. The journalist had obviously been taken to visit the site of the event, and reported seeing two 'chasms' in the moor which had been emptied of all their vegetation, soil and rocks. The larger of the holes was astonishingly big, at least 12 ft (3.5 m) deep and more than 700 yards (650 m) across. 'A channel . . . has been formed quite to the mouth of the gill, down which a most amazing quantity of water was precipitated with a violence and noise of which it is difficult to form an adequate conception,' the paper reported. 'Stones of an immense size and weight were hurried by the torrent more than a mile . . . The torrent at this time presented a breast of seven feet high.'

In his home in Haworth Parsonage, Patrick Bronte – the father of the Bronte sisters – spent a worried evening. The day had hitherto been very fine, and Charlotte Bronte (who was nine at the time), Emily and Anne, together with their brother Branwell, had been out on the moors, looked after by servants. However the party failed to come back at the expected time. Patrick Bronte reported watching a storm build up ('the muttering of distant thunder . . . the frequent flashing of the lightning . . . the gale freshened rapidly') and then described the moment of the bog burst itself:

> I heard a deep, distant explosion, something resembling, and yet something differing from thunder, and I perceived a gentle tremor in the chamber in which I was standing, and in the glass of the window just before me, which, at the time, made an extraordinary impression on my mind.

The Bronte children had, in fact, taken refuge when the storm erupted and – fortunately for English literature – were quite safe. Indeed no lives were lost in the incident, though Ponden farmers suffered from finding their corn fields several feet under water and a number of local bridges were damaged.

Patrick Bronte himself used the bog burst to warn his parishioners of the power of God in a sermon in Haworth church a short while later, taking for his text an appropriate line from Psalm 97: 'The earth saw, and trembled. The hills melted like wax at the presence of the Lord.'

So what caused Stanbury Bog to explode? Various theories have been put forward, including freak weather conditions or the build-up of methane. Patrick Bronte himself had no doubt that the area had suffered from an earthquake, but his theory was dismissed at the time by the *Leeds Mercury*: 'We think the cause of the disruption is to be ascribed . . . simply to the pressure of the accumulated and pent-up waters having become too great,' it reported.

Since September 1824, Stanbury Bog has chosen to revert to its previous quiet way of life. But the question remains, of course, whether an event like the Crow Hill Bog Burst could happen again. Walk this way with care!

WALK 6

TOP WITHENS

DIFFICULTY 🥾 🥾 **DISTANCE 6½ miles (10.5 km)
or 8½ miles (13.7 km) from Haworth**

HAWORTH/	OXENHOPE	TOP	STANBURY	BRONTE	HAWORTH/
PENISTONE	STOOP	WITHENS	MOOR	BRIDGE	PENISTONE
COUNTRY PARK					COUNTRY PARK

MAP OS Explorer OL21, South Pennines

STARTING POINT Penistone Country Park (GR 018361)
or Haworth

PARKING Car park for Penistone Country Park

PUBLIC TRANSPORT Haworth is served by buses from
Keighley, Hebden Bridge and Bradford and also by the Worth
Valley heritage railway from Keighley. In recent years, there have
been infrequent rural bus services (M3, M4) from Keighley and
Haworth which directly pass Penistone Country Park – check
locally for the current situation.

This walk offers a chance
to pay homage to the
landscapes which inspired
the Bronte sisters. The
walk can be undertaken
almost entirely on paths,
although you should
expect wet ground.

▶ If you are starting this walk
from Haworth, take the footpath
beside the churchyard and
parsonage (the former home of
the Brontes), and cross the old
quarries at Penistone.

■ The old quarrying area,
which has now been turned

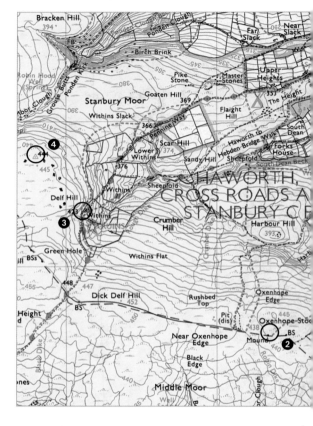

into the Penistone Country Park, helped supply the building stone which was needed for Haworth's development in the nineteenth century. The West End Quarry (the large quarry close to the car parking area recommended for this walk) operated from the 1840s to the 1960s.

▶ From the car park at Penistone Country Park, cross the

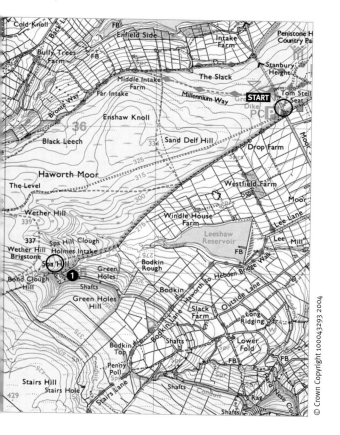

© Crown Copyright 100043293 2004

road and walk up the track which starts beside the old toilet block and heads towards Drop Farm. Beyond Drop Farm continue on to the moorland, taking the path which heads up Spa Hill ❶ and then makes for Oxenhope Stoop

Hill. The path, which is initially well-walked, gradually becomes less defined and wetter.

Eventually the path reaches the hilltop. Continue eastwards and pass the Oxenhope stoop (boundary stone) ❷.

▶ page 74

Top Withens

■ The Oxenhope stoop is one of numerous boundary stones which were erected on the moors. It marks the furthest extent of Haworth parish, on the watershed between the Calder and Aire river basins. The watershed also marks the current local government boundary between Calderdale and Bradford metropolitan authorities.

▶ Continue for a mile (1.6 km) or so past the stoop, on the track which runs along the moor top. In good weather, this stretch of walking offers fine views in both directions, more than compensating for the occasional dampness underfoot.

Turn right when you reach the Pennine Way, and follow the paved path down to the ruined farmhouse which is called Top Withens ❸.

■ Top Withens, as the plaque on the building erected by the Bronte Society will tell you, is reputedly the location which Emily Bronte had in mind for *Wuthering Heights*,

and as such it is one of the most important pilgrimage sites locally for visitors with an interest in the Brontes. The walk from Haworth is well signposted, not only in English but also – to cater for the considerable number of tourists from Japan who come – in Japanese as well (see pages 76–8). Visitors who want the full Bronte Moors bleakness experience, and who are up to the walking, might be better advised to follow the route in this walk, in order to approach Top Withens from the moor side.

▶ Scramble up above Top Withens to find the path which leads off across the moor to the trig point on Stanbury Moor ❹.

■ If you have not already visited the Alcomden Stones (Walk 5), or indeed even if you have, you may want to continue for a short distance beyond the trig point to visit this impressive rocky outcrop. For more about the Alcomden Stones, see pages 62–4.

▶ From the trig point, head off a little north of east across the moor, aiming for the broken-down wall ahead and to your right. The easiest route through the heather and grass is to find the trod which runs down the hillside. Continue until you rejoin the Pennine Way near Scar Hill.

The next objective is Bronte Bridge. Direct moorland tramping across Flaight Hill is possible, but the most straightforward route is to continue on the Pennine Way until you reach the house at Upper Heights, and then follow the footpath signs off to the right, beside a small wood. This next stretch of path is on the route of the Bronte Way long-distance path, which links a number of sites with Bronte connections in West Yorkshire and Lancashire.

■ Perhaps inevitably, the bridge across the South Dean Beck has been given the name Bronte Bridge ❺, while the falls which come down the hillside beyond it to meet the beck are the Bronte Waterfalls. The large rock at the foot of the falls is said to be where Emily Bronte once rested to gain inspiration – so of course it has the name of the Bronte Chair.

It is not surprising therefore if this pleasant area is extremely popular with visitors, particularly on summer weekends.

▶ From here, it's possible to scramble up the side of the Bronte Waterfalls, and then pick a route back across Haworth Moor. The more direct route, however, is to continue along the well-walked footpath at the foot of the hill, using the route also followed by the Bronte Way. Cut back across the moor to Penistone Country Park when you reach Middle Intake Farm.

Turning Japanese

It is not a sight which many walkers expect to see in the Yorkshire countryside. Up on the moors south of Haworth, Stanbury and Ponden, the public footpath signs come in two languages: English, of course, and Japanese.

This is not all. Call in at Haworth tourist information centre, and as well as offering you the usual range of countryside leaflets the staff will be able to sell you an attractive booklet offering details of three walks around the town – with the directions for all the routes carefully set out in Japanese. Try the website www.bradford.gov.uk/countryside, and here too there is information in Japanese available to download.

So what is going on? The story of how Haworth has gone Japanese can be traced back to some inspired thinking by Bradford Council's countryside service, and in particular to one man, David Parsons, who still works for the authority. It was David who, well over ten years ago, noticed that Haworth seemed to be attracting more than its fair share of Japanese visitors, particularly young Japanese women travelling alone and heading off to walk the moorlands above the town. On more than one occasion, he recalls, he encountered some of these visitors up near Top Withens, apparently struggling to find the right paths to follow.

It rapidly became clear that, for many Japanese students of English literature, the journey to Haworth to explore the Bronte countryside was something of a pilgrimage. The Bronte sisters' novels are widely read and studied in Japan, and the romantic setting for the novels – particularly Emily Bronte's powerful *Wuthering Heights* – acted as a magnet for Japanese visitors heading for England. Indeed, Haworth – along with more obvious tourist centres such as Stratford-upon-Avon and Chester – features in a popular Japanese guidebook to England.

At David's suggestion, therefore, the routes to some of the most popular visitor sights for Bronte enthusiasts were colour-coded and an approximate Japanese translation of 'public footpath' added to the finger-boards. The routes include those to the Bronte Waterfalls, to Top Withens (the ruined farmhouse whose setting is considered to be that used by Emily Bronte for *Wuthering Heights*) and to Ponden Hall (used in *Wuthering Heights* as the model for Thrushcross Grange). These steps were quickly followed by the publication of the first translation of the walk routes into Japanese.

It wasn't long before Bradford Council's initiative made the headlines. What began quietly enough, with features in publications such as *The Dalesman*, rapidly became a media sensation, with the story appearing prominently around the world. David Parsons recalls how it became front-page news as far away as New Zealand.

Bronte guide in Japanese

You do not need to be Japanese, of course, to take advantage of a visit to this part of west Yorkshire to renew an interest in the Bronte sisters and their works. Haworth Parsonage, where their father Patrick was the incumbent from 1819 until his death in 1861, is now very well known as the Parsonage Museum, run by the Bronte Society and open for visitors almost every day of the year. The Bronte Society also has a considerable library of resources related to the Bronte family which it makes available to researchers and students.

The Parsonage, which is right next to the graveyard, can seem a forebidding place, particularly in bad weather. Certainly, poor Patrick Bronte cannot have had a very happy time during his period in Haworth: before his own death he had seen his whole family buried. Maria Bronte, his wife, died in 1821 from cancer aged thirty-eight, only a few months after the family had moved to the town. The two eldest daughters, Maria and Elizabeth, both died in 1825 at the ages of eleven and ten respectively. Emily Bronte, who was born in 1818, and her brother Branwell, born in 1817, both died in 1848. A year later the youngest daughter, Anne, also died. Charlotte Bronte outlived her siblings, but died in 1855, still only thirty-eight years old.

Nevertheless, the novels written by Charlotte, Emily and Anne during their time in Haworth live on. Charlotte's best-known works are the novels *Jane Eyre*, *Shirley* and *Villette*. Emily's famous novel *Wuthering Heights* tells the gripping tale of Heathcliff and Cathy, while Anne has left two novels, *Agnes Grey* and *The Tenant of Wildfell Hall*, both of them still read today. All three sisters also wrote poetry.

All the Bronte family except Anne, who died while at Scarborough, are buried in Haworth churchyard.

WALK 7

GREAT EDGE

DIFFICULTY 👟👟👟👟 **DISTANCE** 6½ miles (10.5 km)

WIDDOP (CLOUGH FOOT) — BOULSWORTH HILL — DOVE STONES — GREAT EDGE — WIDDOP

MAP OS Explorer OL21, South Pennines

STARTING POINT Car park at Clough Foot, Widdop (GR 947323)

PARKING In car park beside road

PUBLIC TRANSPORT In recent years, a summer bus service (weekends only) has run to Widdop Gate, about a mile (1.6 km) from the walk start. Enquire locally for the current position.

A walk on to the plateau at the back of Boulsworth Hill, to include the Dove Stones outcrop and Great Edge. Some rough moorland walking.

▶ From the car park at Clough Foot, take the footpath heading off to the north-east across a field, ignoring the Pennine Way route which also leaves the car park at this point. Follow the footpath almost dead straight, and continue in the same direction when the path becomes less well defined. When you reach a well-maintained shooting track, turn left and follow it down to the shooting hut at Greave Clough. Continue on this track as it turns right, to follow the clough upstream.

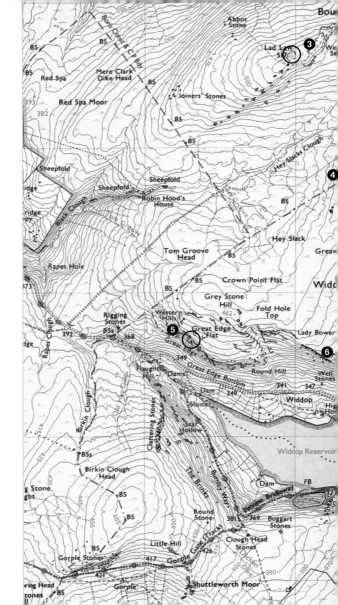

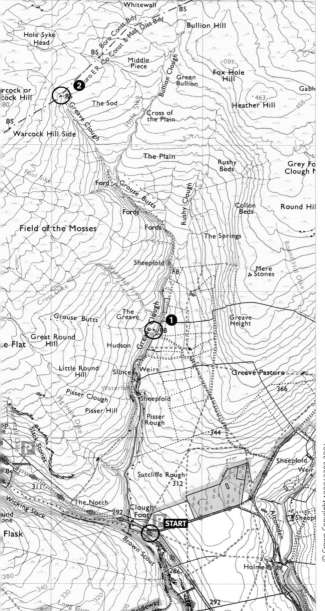

■ Look out under your feet for an old stone bearing the date 1683, which is now being used as part of the surface of the track ❶.

▶ As the shooting track comes to an end, cross the stream and follow the right-hand side of the clough as it heads up towards Boulsworth plateau. There is a trod which can be found for most of the way, though the ground is wet in places.

As you reach the top of the clough ❷, you cross from Yorkshire into Lancashire, and the rocks which mark the summit of Boulsworth Hill (Lad Law) come into sight ahead. It's possible at this point to pick up another trod which runs off south-west, roughly following the county boundary, towards the Dove Stones. However, most people will probably choose to make the slight diversion involved in continuing across the rough moorland ahead to reach Boulsworth summit itself. A number of trods can be found heading across the moorland in the right direction; the ground underfoot is relatively dry.

■ Walk 4 also reaches Boulsworth (for more information see pages 56–9).

A massive weathered stone, forming an almost circular basin, lies just to the eastern side of the trig point on Boulsworth and is well worth inspecting ❸.

▶ From Boulsworth, head south back across the plateau towards Dove Stones. The easiest route is to detour a little to the left, to avoid the wetter ground. You should be able to find a relatively well-defined path, which will make the walking easier. Once you have crossed the plateau, you will be able to pick up another trod leading straight to the Dove Stones ❹.

■ The Dove Stones are a particularly impressive outcrop, especially if they are viewed from the east, when the shape which the rocks make is very striking.

The Dove Stones were previously situated on private land and could be reached only by trespassing. However, visitors have nonetheless come here in the past, drawn it seems by the power of these rocks. Two nineteenth-century folklorists examined the Dove Stones in some detail, and reported discovering examples of cup-and-ring art on rocks facing north-west. More recently, Paul Bennett in *The Old Stones of Elmet* describes his attempt to search for these markings. Many, he concludes, are simply the work of erosion and natural forces, although some he believes are indeed human-made. He adds, 'Two examples in particular stood out . . . Atop of the giant Dove Stone at the end of the ridge is a cup-and-half-ring. Half way along the ridge are three cup-markings in a straight line pointing westwards.' Paul Bennett also suggests that the stones, originally known as the Dew Stones, took their name from the Celtic word for black and not from any ornithological connections.

A colour postcard of the Dove Stones produced by the local Access to Boulsworth Campaign was circulated widely in the House of Commons soon after the election of the Labour government in 1997, to encourage MPs to support access legislation.

▶ From the Dove Stones, a relatively well-defined path heads south-west. While this makes walking easier, it also represents a potentially major environmental problem since the path has been created partly as the result of motor bikes being ridden illegally across this moorland. Access legislation does not, of course, permit trail bikes to be used in sensitive areas such as this but nevertheless the problem of enforcement is difficult.

The path leads straight to another outcrop of rocks on Grey Stone Hill ❺. From here, the obvious route is to turn back south-east to follow Great Edge, the outcrop of rocks which run down the side of the hill, high above Widdop reservoir. There are fine views down over the reservoir to the hills beyond.

▶ page 86

Walshaw reservoirs

■ Widdop reservoir was built to provide water for the people in Halifax, one of a series of local reservoirs which were constructed in the second half of the nineteenth century. Widdop was constructed between 1872 and 1878 by the architect and engineer Edward Bateman. Bateman had been invited to the opening of the Suez Canal a few years earlier, and was influenced by the Egyptian architecture he saw on his visit. Some people detect an Egyptian influence in the design of the water valve tower at the south-east corner of Widdop reservoir.

▶ You can now use any one of a series of trods, some better defined than others, to follow the rock outcrops down Great Edge, and then across and down the Scout and Slack Stones ❻. From here, it's appropriate to cut across the open country to emerge on the Widdop Road just above Clough Foot farmhouse.

■ John Wesley visited Widdop a number of times during his preaching tours in the mid-eighteenth century, describing it after a visit in 1747 as 'a little village in the midst of huge, barren mountains'.

Tradition says that Wesley preached by standing on one of the rocks just above Widdop road, later known as Wesley's Pulpit. The inscription J. W. 1766 was subsequently cut on the rock.

Causey-paths and packhorse trails

In most parts of Britain, the meaning of the word 'causeway' is straightforward – a raised road which provides access across sands to an island, as with the causeway which allows cars at low tide to reach Lindisfarne in Northumberland. In the south Pennines, however, the word has another meaning – a track across the moors which has been paved with stone.

Causeways – or causey-paths, as they are also called locally – criss-cross the moors and hillsides, often waiting to be found in what appear to be the remotest parts of the countryside. They remain as a silent testimony both to the hard physical labour which was expended year after year on their construction and maintenance and to the importance to the local economy for many centuries of the packhorses which used these routes.

Stones are still used today to help walkers keep their feet dry in boggy country, as for example in the work which has recently been undertaken on the Pennine Way between Stoodley Pike and Warland reservoir. But these modern efforts are paltry when compared with the original causey-paths, which demonstrate a high level of engineering competence. Their beautifully set stone slabs, in many cases still in excellent condition today after centuries of use, show the degree of effort which local communities were prepared to put in to keep their transport links in good condition.

To understand why there are causey-paths across the moors of the south Pennines it is necessary to appreciate two things. First, as was mentioned in the introduction, until relatively modern times humans lived on the hillsides, not in the valleys. Second, wool and textiles long played an important role in the local economy, with handloom weaving a feature of life in many upland farmhouses. This necessitated an adequate transport infrastructure of routes and operators to ensure that raw materials could be provided to the weavers and completed cloth taken away to be sold.

Galloway ponies were the answer, and long trains of these ponies, typically a dozen or so but sometimes as many as thirty or forty animals, would be linked together. Each pony could carry about 240 pounds (over 100 kilos) in weight, spread between two panniers. The packhorse trains got a move on, too: in a day, the ponies were able to travel about twenty-five miles (forty kilometres).

Contemporary accounts make it clear that you didn't voluntarily get in the way of a packhorse train in full tilt. Solitary travellers would be expected to leave the paved causey-paths if confronted by an approaching team of ponies, and the hill descents in particular were by all accounts a formidable sight.

It is possible to find references to causey-paths in medieval times, and some of these routes are clearly very ancient. One very long-standing transport artery is the route from Blackshawhead to Mereclough near Burney, which though it has now been turned into a tarmac road recalls its past in its name, the Long Causeway. Salt from the Cheshire salt mines, a particularly important household staple in days when food could not be refrigerated, would have been one of the items carried across the moors on the causey-paths, and the 'salters gates' to be found on modern Ordnance Survey maps recall this trade (gate in this context is being used in the northern and Scandinavian sense of a road or way).

Trading in textiles developed in the south Pennines area from about the fifteenth century, and this would have seen further growth in the use of packhorse trains. Local histories describe the 'dual economy' which became established, whereby families would earn their livelihood by hilltop agriculture and from textiles, in particular from handloom weaving. Not everyone benefited economically, but the fine yeomen's houses which were built in the area in the seventeenth century testify to the fact that some people at least grew wealthy from this early development of industry and commerce.

Later, in the eighteenth century, the turnpike roads were developed while at the very end of the 1700s the Rochdale canal was pushed through the south Pennines between Sowerby Bridge, Rochdale and Manchester. Later still came the railway network. These were the new transport arteries, and the old packhorse routes were no longer needed. But they remain today, as a potent reminder of an important part of the south Pennines' economic history and heritage.

Milestone on an old packhorse trail near Todmorden

WALK 8

HOOF STONES HEIGHT

DIFFICULTY 👢 👢   **DISTANCE 7 miles (11.3 km)**

HURSTWOOD — CANT CLOUGH RESERVOIR — HARE STONES — HOOF STONES HEIGHT — WORSTHORNE MOOR — CANT CLOUGH RESERVOIR — HURSTWOOD

MAP OS Explorer OL21, South Pennines

STARTING POINT Hurstwood village, near Burnley

PARKING In the large visitors' car park at the far end of Hurstwood village (GR 882313)

PUBLIC TRANSPORT Regular bus services (1 and 2) run from Burnley to Worsthorne, ¾ mile (1.2 km) away.

A walk from the Lancashire side of the south Pennine moors up to the Lancashire/ Yorkshire border at Hare Stones and Hoof Stones Height. Upland footpaths, with the option of open moorland walking.

▶ This walk starts at Hurstwood, a small community situated at the end of a no-through-road on the edge of the Pennine moors.

■ Hurstwood has a number of interesting old houses, which help to offset the undistinguished twentieth-century suburban offerings you pass on the way in. Hurstwood Hall was erected, as the stone inscription over the entrance states, in 1579 by Barnard Townley and his young wife Agnes ('Barnardvs Townley et Agnes Uxor Ejus'). Near by is beautiful Spenser's House, which belonged in the seventeenth century to the family of the poet Edmund Spenser. Spenser, who died in 1599 and was buried in poets' corner in Westminster Abbey, is best known as the author of the moral allegory *The Faerie Queene*. He is believed to have lived briefly in Hurstwood during the late 1570s.

▶ From Hurstwood, make your way to Cant Clough reservoir ❶. Walk up the left side of the reservoir, and continue along the well-walked concessionary path up into the moorland.

■ Worsthorne Moor is one of the largest water catchment areas in the south Pennines. The estate is in the ownership of North West Water (United Utilities), who commendably negotiated a public-access agreement covering most of the moorland area in 1956.

▶ On the horizon ahead, unmistakably, are the Hare Stones. Leave the main path, and take one of the smaller paths down into Rams Clough and up the hillside beyond to reach the stones ❷.

■ The Hare Stones are one of the smaller rocky outcrops found in the Widdop area. It may be this author's imagination, but one separate rock close by the Hare Stones seems to resemble a tortoise.

▶ From here, the suggested route turns south, following the Lancashire/Yorkshire border up on to Black Hameldon. This ridge has been well walked, but is peaty and can be wet. Tracks of trail bikes have made the situation much worse. (A longer alternative is to drop down from the Hare Stones on to the moors on the Yorkshire side, passing Gorple Upper reservoir and making for the ruined farmhouse at Raistrick Greave. From here you can follow a footpath across Hoar Side Moor, and then up Noah Dale.)

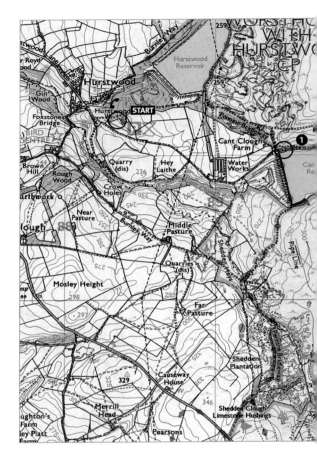

Either way, the target is the trig point at Hoof Stones Height, 1571 ft (479 m) above sea level **3**. There are fine views to enjoy in all directions.

■ Hoof Stones Height is one of the Six Trigs (see pages 136–9). It has given its name to a 'method' or sequence of bells used by bell ringers.

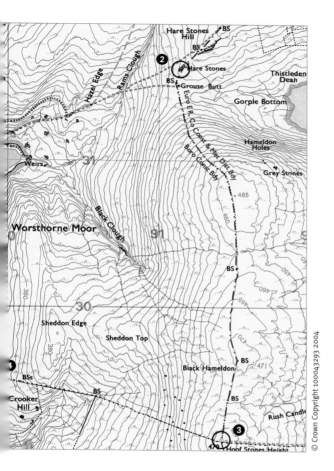

© Crown Copyright 100043293 2004

Here, for the convenience of change ringers, if nobody else, is the notation for Hoof Stones Height:
5×34.1×56×6×4×5×6×7

▶ Turn right at Hoof Stones Height, and drop down the hill. There are plenty of opportunities now for open moorland walking. However, the easier option is to follow the path which runs from the trig point down to meet an old boundary wall near Crooker Hill. At one stage beside the wall is an old boundary stone, marked with a cross.

■ The ground ahead, beside Shedden (or Sheddon) Clough, clearly shows the signs of major workings ❹. These are the 'hushings' which were created in the seventeenth and eighteenth centuries to extricate the limestone which could be found here. The limestone ended up in this part of Lancashire as a result of the Ice Age, when an ice sheet stretched down from the limestone area in what is now the Yorkshire Dales and carried the limestone with it.

The technique used to obtain the limestone was to scour away (or 'hush') the surface soil and other matter around limestone boulders, using the power of water. This entailed building a complex series of water channels, ponds and dams which enabled enough water to be harnessed for the operation. When all was prepared, the water would be released down the valley, taking with it the unwanted clays and sands.

The limestone itself was then fired in lime kilns, to be turned into lime which was used both in agriculture and in the construction of buildings. The limestone hushings were abandoned more than 200 years ago, but in recent years one lime kiln has been reconstructed. It is possible to follow a trail prepared for visitors through the heart of the hushings area.

▶ Before Shedden Clough, a concessionary path is met. This runs northwards across Worsthorne Moor, back to the dam at Cant Clough reservoir.

■ At Cant Clough, the route briefly joins the Pennine Bridleway. This long-distance trail, designed especially for horse-riders and mountain bikers (although also available for walkers), parallels the Pennine Way, generally on somewhat lower ground.

When fully opened, the Pennine Bridleway will run from Middleton Top in Derbyshire to Byrness in Northumberland. The southern section opened in 2004, following the opening two years earlier of the very first part of the Bridleway, the Mary Towneley Loop. This 47-mile (75-km) circular trail around the moors of the south and west Pennines is named in memory of Mary Towneley, a keen horsewoman who used to live in Cliviger, near Burnley. She had campaigned for many years for the bridleway network in northern Britain to be improved, but it was a pioneering long-distance horse ride the length of the Pennines which she undertook in 1985 with two friends – in places along old tracks which had not been ridden for over 100 years – which helped to create the momentum which later was to lead to the Pennine Bridleway. Mary Towneley was delighted to see the Countryside Agency develop the idea, although sadly she died before the Bridleway was opened.

▶ From Cant Clough, return to Hurstwood.

Twite Aid

For some people, the twite is a small brown bird, inconspicuous and elusive. But for others it is not just any small brown bird. This is *Carduelis flavirostris*, sometimes called the Pennine finch, the upland cousin of the linnet and a bird with a particular liking for life on the south Pennine moors.

The twite breeds in relatively large numbers in Scotland, but in England the vast majority of twite can be found only in what the RSPB has dubbed the 'twite triangle', the moors which lie between Huddersfield, Rochdale, Burnley and Keighley. Calderdale's moors, in particular, seem to be a favourite spot for the birds.

Sadly, however, this is not a good time to be a twite. The British twite population has fallen significantly over the past hundred years, partly because of changes in farming practice. In the south Pennines the decline in recent years has been troubling. A survey in 1999 suggested that the numbers of Pennine breeding birds could be down to as few as 225 pairs, about half the 415 or so pairs estimated in a similar 1990 survey.

For the RSPB, the seriousness of this decline in numbers demanded action: it was time to start a rescue mission, and RSPB Twite Aid was duly launched. This initiative, in conjunction with farmers, landowners and local authorities, aims in the longer term to encourage farmers to change their hay-making practice, cutting the fields later and avoiding the use of fertilizer. There are financial incentives, under the Countryside Stewardship Scheme, to help farmers move towards these more twite-friendly farming practices.

In the immediate future, however, other measures are needed. Twite Aid is currently roping in volunteers and RSPB staff to go out on to the moors and help the nesting birds by leaving extra food out for them.

Food in this context means seeds, particularly of sorrel but also of upland meadow flowers such as buttercups, dandelions, meadow-grass and thistles. The birds nest on the moors themselves, in areas of bracken or heather, but rely on the hay meadows adjacent to moors for a ready supply of these seeds. So farmers who harvest early for silage production – or councils

Twite – inconspicuous and elusive

who mow roadside verges before flowers have seeded – remove an important source of food for the nesting birds.

Anyone spending any time on the south Pennine moors is likely to walk through areas where twite can be found. It can be a frustrating matter, however, trying to spot one. The bird, which is smaller than a sparrow, is unassuming and will not willingly draw attention to itself. It is also predominantly brown: it has a tawny-coloured face, breast and back, which is streaked with dark brown. The male bird breaks this dominant theme by having a pink rump, but unfortunately this feature is usually difficult to see.

The answer, according to the RSPB, can be to use one's ears rather than eyes. The twite gets its name from the sound it makes, a hoarse nasal buzzing which can sound a little like 'twi-eeete' or 'dwy-eeete'. It is this sound which can provide the proof that twite are in the vicinity. When flying, the twite also has another chattering call, which has been described as sounding like 'tup-up-up'.

The south Pennine moors provide a home for twite to raise two broods of chicks, the first in mid-May to mid-June and the second in mid-June to mid-July. Later in the year, after the chicks are fledged, most of the Pennine twite fly across to East Anglia, to nest on salt marshes in the Wash and in Suffolk and Essex, with some also crossing the North Sea to the Netherlands. Small flocks of twite remain on the Pennine moors throughout the winter, however.

WALK 9

CHURN MILK JOAN

DIFFICULTY 🥾 🥾 🥾   **DISTANCE 10 miles (16 km)**

OLD TOWN (HARE AND HOUNDS PH) — CHURN MILK JOAN — SALTONSTALL — WARLEY MOOR — FLY FLATS — HIGH BROWN KNOLL — OLD TOWN

MAP OS Explorer OL21, South Pennines

STARTING POINT Hare and Hounds pub, Old Town, Hebden Bridge (GR 005280)

PARKING On road beside pub

PUBLIC TRANSPORT Buses from Hebden Bridge and, at the time of writing, some through buses from Halifax

This is a fine moorland walk, which crosses the heather from the Calder valley to the beautiful valley of Luddenden Dean and then explores the countryside beyond. A chance to pay a visit to Churn Milk Joan, a singular lady of the moors.

▶ The walk begins at Old Town, above Hebden Bridge in the upper Calder valley. Leave the pub to walk along the road, heading south-east. After a few hundred yards (metres), immediately as the fields on the left give way to open country, turn left up the footpath to strike the Calderdale Way. You should turn right here.

Follow the Calderdale Way footpath round the side of the Mount Skip golf club, and stay

▶ page 102

on this well-marked path as it climbs round the side of Crow Hill. In due course, a single standing stone comes into sight, just off the path to the left (GR 021277) ❶.

■ Although not marked as such on maps, this stone is known as Churn Milk Joan. There's a tradition, as you pass, of leaving a coin or two in the hollow at the top of the stone. Replacing coins already there with the same or a larger sum brings good luck, it's said.

This tradition was commemorated in a poem (also called 'Churn Milk Joan') by the former poet laureate Ted Hughes, who grew up down the hill in Mytholmroyd. He suggests that, originally, the stone was used as a place where farmers left milk for local villagers, who would leave the money which they owed in exchange in Churn Milk Joan's hollow. If you prefer a more pagan origin for your folk traditions – which you might, if the weather's bad – it's easy to imagine the coins as an appeasement to the spirit of the moors.

Quite how the stone got its name is unclear, though one story tells of a milkmaid who lived in the Mount Skip pub near by (now private houses) who was attacked by foxes while on the moors in a snowstorm. Ted Hughes has none of this, however, arguing in his poem that the stone's name should be Churn Milk jamb.

In reality, the stone was probably put up in about 1600 to help resolve a boundary dispute between the lords of the two manors, Wadsworth and Midgley.

▶ Leave the Calderdale Way just before Churn Milk Joan, and head north-east from the stone through the heather. (There are a number of choices of route; the easiest walking is by the most obvious track.) Shortly ahead, you will see the valley of Luddenden Dean spread out before you.

■ This part of the moor is rich in mesolithic (middle

Stone Age) sites, including earthworks and standing stones.

▶ Turn left along the moorside to follow a well-worn path, which turns right shortly to drop down the side of the hill. Follow the paths down to the valley bottom, and turn left on to the road here to arrive at a gatehouse, built in the nineteenth century for the house at Castle Carr, further up the valley. At the gatehouse ❷, turn right up the road and shortly afterwards turn left on to a footpath heading up the hills. Clamber up until you reach another tarmac road, just beyond a house ❸.

The aim now is to make for the open moorland of Warley Moor, east of Upper Dean Head reservoir. One way on to this land is to take the right of way for a short way towards the Rocking Stone and Slade and then turn left ❹, picking up the conduit (shown on OS maps) as it contours around the side of curiously named Too To Hill. This is roughish walking.

This route offers views down to the wooded head of the

Luddenden valley, and to the string of reservoirs. Opposite, on the other side of the valley, can be seen the ruins of Castle Carr.

Alternatively, stay on the footpath to the Rocking Stone outcrop. Despite its name, the main stone is resolutely stationary, but in good weather commands a fine view. From here, cut back to the west, along a line of grouse butts.

■ Castle Carr may look like a genuine medieval castle but appearances are deceptive. The house was built in an antique style in the 1850s for a local worthy, Captain Joseph Priestley Edwards. It passed through several hands before becoming dilapidated, and the majority of the house was demolished in the 1960s. The ruins you can see are more or less all that remains of the house.

When Halifax Water Corporation acquired the nearby land to construct reservoirs, a series of water features, including a spectacular fountain 130 ft (40 m) high, were

▶ page 106

Churn Milk Joan

constructed for Castle Carr by way of compensation. This fountain is still in working order, and is usually operated once or twice a year, to coincide with the times when the grounds of Castle Carr are opened to the public. (Castle Carr itself is on private land, not covered by access legislation.) In full spate the fountain is a very impressive sight and it is well worth checking locally for future dates when it can be admired. (Calderdale tourist information offices normally can supply details.)

The construction of Castle Carr controversially extinguished the *de facto* access rights which the public had previously enjoyed to the upper Luddenden valley. A legal hearing relating to disputed legal rights of way in the Castle Carr area took place in London in 1898.

▶ Continue along the hillside above Upper Dean Head reservoir and the upper Luddenden Brook valley. Although the path becomes less and less well used, it can be followed without too much difficulty. You will arrive in due course at a more well-defined track.

■ About 100 yards (100 m) before arriving at the track, look out for a small stone to your left, a few yards (metres) away. This resembles a gravestone, and bears the inscription 'A sinner saved by grace'. It may or may not be a grave, but it seems possible that it was carved by one of the navvies employed during the nineteenth century in the work of constructing the reservoir.

▶ Turn right here and almost immediately you will arrive at the retaining earth wall of a large reservoir. Although described on maps as Warley Moor reservoir it is better known locally as Fly Flats, or Fly Flat ❺.

■ The local sailing club makes use of Fly Flats, and the wind can certainly blow strongly across the water up here. The reservoir is sited about 1300 ft (410 m) above sea level.

▶ At Fly Flats clamber up the bank to reach the waterside. Here turn left and follow the bank of the reservoir along a track. At the end of the reservoir ❻ turn left again, to find the path which runs south-westwards to follow the side of Catchwater Drain, one of the drainage channels constructed at the same time as the reservoir.

The Catchwater Drain path contours around the hillside, now on the opposite side of the upper Luddenden valley. This path, although used informally for many years, is not a right of way but can now be legitimately used because of access rights.

If you enjoy rough moorland walking, you can head off westwards when the path turns around the top of Spa Clough ❼, to make for the rocky outcrop known as Winny Stone. From here, a trod can be picked up, running southerly. Alternatively (for easier walking), stay on the Catchwater Drain path for another mile (1.6 km) or so, until

it turns back north-westwards, to climb up to the trig point at High Brown Knoll ❽.

■ High Brown Knoll is 1453 ft (443 m) high. On a clear day, there are views eastwards towards the television transmitter at Emley Moor, as well as towards the power stations at Drax and Ferrybridge, well beyond Leeds.

▶ From High Brown Knoll follow the main path southwards, dropping down across the moor. Once you approach the edge of the moor, you will have a choice of a number of footpaths to take you back across the fields beyond to the starting point of the walk. One option is to find the unsealed road which runs down (from just south of Old Hold Farm) past a number of buildings to emerge directly opposite the pub.

■ Although the signs above the door proclaim the name of the pub as the Hare and Hounds, it is better known locally as the Lane Ends.

Robin Hood

To the rest of the world it might seem a forlorn cause, but there are Yorkshire people still determined to prove that Nottinghamshire has done the dirty in claiming Robin Hood as its own – and that the historical Robin Hood was a native of God's own county, Yorkshire.

Periodically, Yorkshire seizes the chance to get its own back in the Robin Hood heritage stakes. In 2004, for example, it was announced that the name chosen for the new civilian airport on the site of the former RAF station at Finningley near Doncaster was to be the Robin Hood Doncaster/Sheffield airport. Robin Hood, a bemused public was told, had spent most of his life in the Doncaster area. Nottingham was not amused.

Yorkshire's claims to Robin Hood may not be entirely fanciful. As well as Robin Hood's Bay, the well-known village on the north Yorkshire coast near Whitby, there are Robin Hood names to be found on the map across Yorkshire, including places near Huddersfield, York and Wakefield. There is also a long-standing legend that the outlaw met his death at the hands of a treacherous nun at Kirklees Priory, north-east of Huddersfield. Robin Hood's Grave is marked on maps near what is now Kirklees Hall, just south of Junction 25 of the M62.

But Robin Hood clearly travelled widely, if names on maps are to be trusted. Walkers following the routes in this book will find that they have a number of opportunities to pay their respects to the elusive outlaw.

Robin Hood's Bed is a large millstone grit boulder high up on the moors at Blackstone Edge (GR 973162), just south of the trig point. It is on the route suggested for Walk 12, and is clearly shown on OS maps. It offers a very fine view down from the Pennine edge, towards Oldham and Rochdale.

Further north, on Midgley Moor north-east of Hebden Bridge, is a boulder known as Robin Hood's Penny Stone (GR 019282). This is not shown on modern OS maps, but Robin Hood enthusiasts should start looking close to the Miller's Grave earthworks on the moor, which are marked on maps. The suggested route for Walk 9 crosses this part of Midgley Moor.

According to Paul Bennett in his book *The Old Stones of Elmet*, there was another Robin Hood's Penny Stone not far from Midgley, at Wainstalls in the Luddenden valley, and a small rock outcrop called Robin Hood Stones close to what is still the Robin Hood pub in Cragg Vale near Mytholmroyd. This is conveniently positioned for walkers thinking of tackling Walk 10.

Further north again is another Robin Hood's Stone, south of Addingham High Moor and about two miles (three kilometres) south of the suggested route for Walk 2.

Finally, there is Robin Hood's House to be found near Boulsworth Hill, the directions to which are given in the instructions for Walk 4. But Yorkshire folk should be careful – this ruined house is just across the county border, in Lancashire. Could it be that Robin Hood was a Lancastrian all along?

WALK 10

ON HIGHER HOUSE MOOR

DIFFICULTY 👟 👟 **DISTANCE 8 miles (13 km)**

| CRAGG VALE | HIGHER HOUSE MOOR | HOLDER STONES | STOODLEY PIKE | CRAGG VALE |

MAP OS Explorer OL21, South Pennines

STARTING POINT Cragg Vale, beside Hinchcliffe Arms pub
(GR 999232)

PARKING Some parking is possible at the edge of the road
beyond the Hinchcliffe Arms pub. (No parking in pub car park.)

PUBLIC TRANSPORT Regular buses from Hebden Bridge
and Mytholmroyd

This walk takes in the moors south of the Calder valley, and includes a visit to the well-known landmark Stoodley Pike. A little rough moorland walking, with the option of more by choice.

▶ The first objective on this walk is a shooting hut (shown on OS maps as a shooting box, GR 991218). From Cragg Vale take the tarmac farm track almost opposite the Hinchcliffe Arms, heading south. The maps show a choice of two rights of way to reach the moor at Cove Hill; the lower path heads through woodland and is particularly attractive.

From Cove Hill, follow the line of the right of way south-westwards to the shooting hut (the path is indistinct, and it can be helpful to take a rough compass bearing ❶.

From here, scramble up the clough, heading west. After about ½ mile (0.8 km), you will abruptly reach the footpath which has been offered as a concessionary path for a number of years by Yorkshire Water.

If you fancy further moorland walking, it's possible to cross this path and head across rough ground towards the trig point at Little Holder Stones. Another tempting option is to make a small diversion to the right (northwards), to visit the Two Lads. These are prominent cairns built on substantial rocks, standing up on the moors like a set of salt and pepper pots ❷.

■ There is a story – similar to that of the Lad o' Crow Hill (see page 65) – that these two cairns mark the site where two local boys perished in a snowstorm. However, it is likely that the Two Lads were originally used as boundary markers.

The cairns have certainly been in this position for more than 200 years, but may be much older. This stretch of moorland was historically in Sowerby township, and the word Sowerby can, with some difficulty, be seen on the more easterly of the two rocks (the word is spread over two lines). Sowerby township was divided into a number of hamlets, and according to local historian Stephen Welsh it is possible that the Two Lads once marked the dividing line between Withens and Turley Holes hamlets.

There appear to be cup markings on one of the rocks.

▶ If you choose to remain on the Yorkshire Water path, follow it as it heads off, high above the side of Withens Clough reservoir, in a roughly westerly direction. The Holder Stones soon come into sight, just to the left of the path. It is a simple matter to cross the drainage channel and clamber up to the Holder Stones ❸, and only a short diversion further south to reach the trig point found at the Little Holder Stones.

▶ page 114

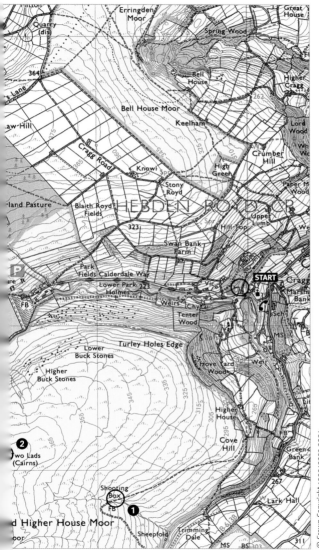

© Crown Copyright 100043293 2004

Find your way either back to the Yorkshire Water path or across the moor to the Pennine Way north of Warland reservoir. Then continue on the Pennine Way as it heads straight across Coldwell Hill.

■ Walkers tackling the Pennine Way from Edale in Derbyshire north to Kirk Yetholm on the Scottish border normally reach this stretch of the path on their third day of walking, having tackled the peaty bogs of Kinder, Bleaklow and Black Hill further south. According to Wainwright, they will have walked 38 miles (61 km) from Edale; there are a further 232 miles (373 km) left to go.

▶ The Pennine Way crosses an important old packhorse route (now followed by the Calderdale Way footpath) at Withens Gate ❹. The junction of the paths is marked by a particularly high stoop (stone marker post). Although the suggested route here is to continue along the Pennine Way to Stoodley Pike obelisk, the fascinating stone called Te Deum is only 100 yards (100 m) away to the right, along the Calderdale Way. It can be found just the other side of the first farm gate ❺.

■ This stone is inscribed with a cross, and (on one side) the first three words of the famous Latin hymn, *Te Deum Laudamus* ('We praise Thee, O God').

The local story attached to this stone is that it was a resting place for coffins, in the days when there was no church at Cragg Vale and bodies had to be carried across the moors to Todmorden for burial.

Beyond Te Deum are the uninviting waters of Withens Clough reservoir, built to provide water for the town of Morley and completed in 1894. A number of farmhouses were lost under the waters.

▶ Carry on along the Pennine Way to Stoodley Pike ❻.

■ Stoodley Pike has been a prominent landmark high

above the Calder valley since it was first constructed in 1814–15 as a 'peace monument' to commemorate the end of the Napoleonic Wars. The original obelisk fell in 1854 (some people point to the strange coincidence that this happened at the very time when Britain and Russia were about to declare war in the Crimea) and was rebuilt in its present shape in 1856 after the Crimean War was over. The obelisk is 120 ft (36 m) high. It is worth braving the pitch darkness inside to climb up the steps to the viewing platform.

▶ From the Pike, take one of the footpaths down the moorside to Withens Clough, and then follow the road back down to Cragg Vale. Or, for a slightly longer walk, head eastwards to pick up the walled Dick's Lane, to emerge on to the open moorland of Erringden Moor and Bell House Moor. From here, there is a choice of footpaths and tracks back to the centre of Cragg Vale.

■ Erringden Moor and Bell House Moor, together with Edge End Moor to the west, and the hillside east to Cragg Vale and south to Withens Clough, were a medieval deer park, enclosed by a deep ditch and an earthbank on which was built a palisade. Traces of the ditch can still be tracked down, even though the deer park lost its paling fence in the fifteenth century and the park was distributed into various landholdings.

The deer park fence is still remembered by the street name Palace House Road in Hebden Bridge, the first word of which is a corruption of 'palis' or palisade.

Stoodley Pike monument

With the Chartists on Blackstone Edge

Walk the south Pennines today above Littleborough on the moorland running down from Blackstone Edge to the M62 motorway and it's easy to find solitude. But turn the clock back to the 1840s, and you could have found the Blackstone Edge moors positively packed with people. The moors close to the White House inn on the Ripponden–Littleborough trans-Pennine route were the gathering point for some of the largest Chartist rallies in this part of the north of England.

Chartism has been described by the historian Asa Briggs as 'the greatest movement of popular protest in British history'. It was certainly the first large-scale independent working-class political movement, and – perhaps not surprisingly – it struck a deep chord in the Pennine towns and villages in this part of Yorkshire and Lancashire, where industrialization was rapidly transforming the old ways of life and, in the process, bringing great distress to the large numbers of handloom weavers. Chartists were very active in places such as Halifax, Huddersfield and

Burnley, but also in smaller towns such as Todmorden, where one man later recalled how people would be out lining the streets to await the weekly arrival of the Chartist newspaper, the *Northern Star*.

Chartists were united in their campaign for the Charter, with its famous six demands for, among other things, universal suffrage, equal electoral districts, secret ballots and payment for MPs – the cornerstones, in other words, of a modern

Chartist meeting at Basin Stone, Todmorden

electoral democracy. The Charter's six points were first published in 1838 and the eleven years from then until 1848, when the third national petition to Parliament was rejected and an unsuccessful Chartist demonstration held in London, are seen by historians as the central period of the movement. Chartism built on earlier popular movements (including the Luddite struggles a generation earlier, which had their focus in towns near Huddersfield), and left an important legacy for later nineteenth-century social movements.

The Chartists used common land and the moors adjacent to their towns for their meetings: an illustration survives, for example, of a Chartist rally at the Basin Stone, a large moorland boulder above Todmorden. But for several years in the 1840s, Blackstone Edge became a particularly important venue. It had the benefit of being within easy reach of industrial towns on both sides of the Pennines, and enthusiastic supporters of the Chartist movement walked there from places such as Halifax, Ripponden, Todmorden and Hebden Bridge in one direction, and from Oldham, Rochdale, Bacup and Heywood in the other.

One of the largest gatherings at Blackstone Edge took place on Sunday 2 August 1846, when according to the *Northern Star* up to 30,000 attended. As today at political demonstrations, the occasion would have been both colourful and noisy, with banners being brought from each of the towns represented. The event was commemorated in a song composed by Ernest Jones, who was also one of the speakers at the rally.

The opening verse of 'The Blackstone-Edge Gathering' describes an experience familiar today to anyone who reaches Blackstone Edge from the Yorkshire side as the view down to Rochdale and Manchester suddenly opens up – although these days the morning sun is no longer blocked by the smoke from textile mills:

O'er plains and cities far away,
All lorn and lost the morning lay,
When sunk the sun at break of day
In smoke of mill and factory.

But waved the wind on Blackstone height
A standard of the broad sunlight,
And sung, that morn, with trumpet might,
A sounding song of Liberty.

Jones goes on to praise the members of 'England's true nobility' who had gathered on Blackstone Edge, and ends his verses in stirring fashion:

How distant cities quaked to hear,
When rolled from that high hill the cheer,
Of – Hope to slaves! To tyrants fear!
And God and man for liberty!

The Blackstone Edge rally of 1846 was, in fact, the first time that Jones had addressed a mass audience. He was unusual in that he came from a higher social class than most Chartist supporters (his father was a retired army officer), and he had trained as a barrister before, through a series of misfortunes, becoming bankrupt. He converted to Chartism, and first became active in the campaign a year before the rally. Jones rapidly became one of the most popular Chartist leaders and orators (he stood, unsuccessfully, for Parliament on a Chartist platform in Halifax in 1847), but he was also well known as a poet. 'The Blackstone-Edge Gathering' was printed in the *Northern Star*, and was designed by Jones to be sung to a popular tune of the day.

WALK 11

GREAT MANSHEAD

DIFFICULTY 🥾 🥾 🥾 🥾   **DISTANCE 7 miles (11.3 km)**

| CRAGG VALE ROAD | MANSHEAD END | GREAT MANSHEAD | HIGHER HOUSE MOOR | WHITE HOLME RESERVOIR | CRAGG VALE ROAD |

MAP OS Explorer OL21, South Pennines

STARTING POINT Lay-by on Cragg Vale road, north-east of Blackstone Edge reservoir (GR 977187)

PARKING In lay-by

PUBLIC TRANSPORT A regular bus service (528) between Halifax/Ripponden and Rochdale/Littleborough passes less than ½ mile (0.8 km) away. In recent years, a grant-supported rural bus service (900) between Hebden Bridge/Mytholmroyd and Ripponden/Huddersfield has travelled up Cragg Vale road – check locally for the current situation.

A walk on both sides of the upper Cragg Vale valley. Stretches of challenging moorland walking.

▶ From the lay-by, cross the stile and follow the side of Cold Laughton Drain north-eastwards, using the trod on the left of the drainage channel. As the drain turns to the east, head off across the open moor to the derelict farm on Collin Hill, below Manshead End ❶. From the derelict house, carry on up the side of Manshead End to reach the cairn at the top. This is tussocky ground, which can be very hard going.

■ The Manshead area has yielded archaeological remains which suggest that the hill was used in mesolithic and neolithic times ❷. There is evidence that flint working took place here. Several flint arrowheads have been found, as well as a stone axehead.

▶ From Manshead End, pick up the concessionary footpath instituted by Yorkshire Water and opened in 1993. The path leads to the trig point (1368 ft/417 m), and then on to Great Manshead Hill.

■ Over to the south lies Baitings reservoir, built from 1948 to 1956 and one of the last reservoirs to be constructed on these south Pennine moors. The concrete dam holds back up to 775 million gallons.

This reservoir is also fed from Cragg Vale by water which is taken under Great Manshead Hill through the Manshead Tunnel, hundreds of feet below you. The tunnel was constructed in the early 1960s, and is about 1½ miles

(2.5 km) long. It links Withens Clough reservoir with Baitings, enabling an extra 2.9 million gallons a day to be taken into Baitings. Manshead Tunnel is one of a number of similar underground water tunnels built across the moors.

▶ Follow the path down the side of Great Manshead Hill. From here, it's possible to cross the moor down to the Cragg Vale road. This is also hard going, particularly the final stretch down to the road. (An easier but longer alternative would be to follow the footpath north-west, and then pick up the road from Sowerby near Sykes Farm.)

At the junction of the Cragg Vale and Sowerby roads ❸, you should take the tarmac bridleway beside the farm buildings down to Washford Bridge.

■ The small river which flows down Cragg Vale is variously known as Elphin Brook, Cragg Brook and Turvin Beck. The sluice gate visible from Washford Bridge is a reminder that it has been

▶ page 126

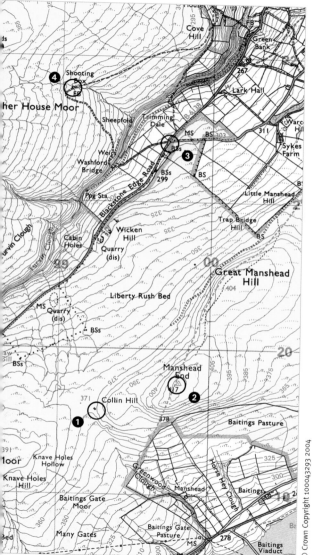

© Crown Copyright 100043293 2004

many years since the river has been allowed to make its own way down to the Calder without human interference. The water, as in so many rivers in the area, was harnessed early in the Industrial Revolution to provide energy to power the textile mills. At least nine mills were built alongside the Elphin Brook. One, a little way to the north of Washford Bridge, was Turvin Mill, which was built in 1808. It had a 10-horsepower water wheel, and in 1833 employed fifty-seven workers, more than half of whom were children.

The conditions in the Cragg Vale mills, particularly for children, seem to have been especially poor. One clergyman was reported as saying, 'If there was one place in England that needed legislative interference, it was this place, for they work fifteen and sixteen hours a day frequently and sometimes all night. Oh! It is a murderous system and the mill owners are the pest and disgrace of society.'

Perhaps unsurprisingly, the Cragg Vale mills were attacked in August 1842, during the so-called Plug Riots. This was a period of considerable industrial unrest across northern England. In the Calder valley area, men armed with bludgeons rendered the mills inoperable by raking the fires out of the mill boilers and removing the plugs. In Cragg Vale, there were also attempts to breach the dams in the small reservoirs, which had been built upstream of the mills to allow a sufficient head of water to be collected to drive the mills.

▶ From Washford Bridge, find your way up the side of Higher House Moor. An initially good path soon deteriorates into a series of faint trods. It's possible to aim for the shooting hut (also visited in Walk 10) ❹, or to by-pass it by keeping on the left-hand side of the clough.

Keep climbing up through the bracken, heather and grasses for at least ½ mile (0.8 km). Finally, and unexpectedly, you will arrive at the well-trodden concessionary footpath which circles the high moors and its reservoirs ❺. From here, the easiest way back to the start of the walk is to follow this path left, along the side of White House Drain, round the top of Little Moor Clough and then along the retaining wall of White Holme reservoir ❻. Alternatively, for more open moorland walking, cross the path and the drainage channel to explore the upper section of Higher House Moor. The stones known as the Wool Pack, north of White Holme reservoir, are one obvious place to explore.

Return along the track built by North West Water (United Utilities) to the starting point.

DOG HILL AND CAT MOSS

DIFFICULTY 👢 👢   **DISTANCE** 7½ miles (12 km)

WHITE   BLACKSTONE   GREEN WITHENS   DOG HILL   WHITE
HOUSE PH   EDGE   RESERVOIR   HOUSE PH

MAP OS Explorer OL21, South Pennines

STARTING POINT White House pub, on
Littleborough–Ripponden road (GR 968178)

PARKING In car park below pub

PUBLIC TRANSPORT A regular bus service (528) between
Halifax/Ripponden and Rochdale/Littleborough passes the
White House.

**Blackstone Edge, Robin
Hood's Bed and the
moorland down to M62.
Some rough walking.**

▶ From the White House pub,
follow the route of the Pennine
Way on to Blackstone Edge Moor.
Continue to follow the Pennine
Way, turning left when the paved
'Roman Road' is reached, after
about ⅔ mile (1 km).

■ The trans-Pennine
crossing at Blackstone Edge
has been an important
transport link for centuries
❶. Perhaps not surprisingly,
given the climb from
Littleborough of close to
800 ft (250 m), it has also on
occasions been problematic.

Many local histories
recount the report given in
1698 of the crossing of
Blackstone Edge by traveller

and writer Celia Fiennes. She wrote, 'Then I came to Blackstonedge, noted all over England for a dismal high precipice and steep in the ascent and descent on either end . . . its a moist ground soe as is usual on these high hills; they stagnate the air and hold mist and rains almost perpetually.' As mentioned earlier, Daniel Defoe also, in 1724, experienced terrible weather in the Pennines, though it is likely he chose a route slightly further south.

Celia Fiennes wrote that she travelled on a 'causey' across Blackstone Edge. The paved causey still exists, and is marked on OS maps as 'Roman Road' though this attribution is debated, sometimes heatedly. Some argue that the paving is more likely to be the remains of an old packhorse route, built long after Romans had left the Pennines. Against this is the argument that the straightness of the line of the route is much more typical of Roman road construction

than packhorse trails. The nature of the paving, too, is not typical of other packhorse causeys in the area.

Either way, the remains of this road are very impressive. The substantial paved area begins abruptly, at about 1000 ft (300 m). The paved area is about 16 ft (5 m) wide, with the distinctive stone 'gutter' in the centre of the paved area. The road climbs steadily, at a maximum gradient of almost 1 in 4.

This direct route up and over Blackstone Edge was only the first of several routes created. The current route followed by the main road past the White House was established in the late eighteenth century, when it was a turnpike. It curves its way up the side of the hillside, trying to avoid very steep gradients. Before that an earlier turnpike had taken a different route up the hill, passing through the hamlet of Lydgate and from there up the hill by way of what is now the bridleway running parallel to the road.

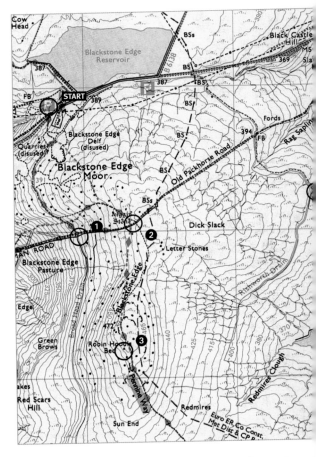

▸ Continue up the Pennine Way to the Aiggin Stone, and turn right.

■ The Aiggin Stone ❷ is an ancient standing stone,

presumably erected as a stoop. It has the remains of a cross and the letters 'IT' marked on its face.

When Wainwright walked

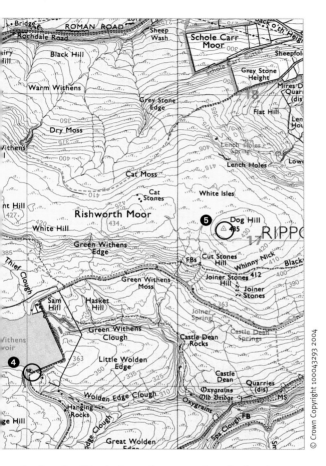

© Crown Copyright 100043293 2004

the Pennine Way in the 1960s, he commented on the fact that the stone was lying on its side and added, 'It seems odd that the local archaeologists have not sought to re-erect it.' In 1997, the Littleborough Civil Trust and Littleborough Lions did just this.

▶ page 134

Green Withens reservoir

The origin of the name Aiggin has been much debated. One theory is that it could come from the French word *aiguille*, a needle. Another suggestion is that it may come from the Latin word *aggerare*, to heap up.

▶ Still on the Pennine Way, continue along the Blackstone Edge rock outcrops, to the trig point. The large flat rock which you will find shortly past this point is known as Robin Hood's Bed (see page 109) ❸.

From here, it's possible to cut eastwards across open country, making for the right-hand side of Green Withens reservoir. To avoid wet ground, keep a little away from the reservoir edge. (If you want to circumvent this stretch of moorland walking, another possible route would be to follow the Pennine Way south to the M62, and then take another path back up to Green Withens ❹.)

Beyond Green Withens clubhouse, turn north over the reservoir dam and then head east, following the track which you will find running alongside a water-drainage channel. This is a well-walked concessionary footpath.

The next target is Dog Hill ❺, which is the highest ground in the area at about 1427 ft (435 m). A path runs up to the trig point on the top of the hill.

■ The M62 makes its presence felt on this part of the walk, both visually and audibly. The motorway was planned in the early 1960s, and work began in 1968. Writer Keith Parry in his book *Trans-Pennine Heritage* reports on some of the problems the engineers had to face: 'The peat covering on the moor was up to 20 ft deep and it was found that the only way to remove it was to dig a vertical shaft and then excavate horizontally (excavators working on the surface sank immediately). Well over 60 in of rain fell in one year (and 12 in over one month), turning the whole area into a quagmire. One of the engineers remarked that it was the only place he had ever worked where it actually rained upwards!'

► From Dog Hill, head down across the damp ground of Cat Moss. The easiest route back to the comfort of the White House is to make use of the concessionary footpath which snakes around the side of Warm Withens Hill **❻**, and then across to Blackstone Edge reservoir.

Possible Roman road, Blackstone Edge

The Six Trigs

In the days when map-making required long hard days in the field and skilled surveyors experienced in the science of triangulation, the Ordnance Survey needed its network of familiar four-foot (1.25-m) high white concrete pillars, located on Britain's mountains and hills. Staff would struggle up the hills, erect their theodolites on the pillars and use them to calculate the exact angles to the places they were surveying.

Map-making has moved on, and now satellite technology has greatly improved the speed and accuracy with which maps can be compiled and updated. But the network of trig points, some now losing their white paint, remains.

Concrete pillars on hilltops might originally have seemed ugly. Long familiarity, however, has turned trig points into old friends for most walkers, and they provide convenient objectives for walks. Link several trig points together and they also create challenging day-long walks, worthy of the fittest outdoor enthusiast.

And so it is with the Six Trigs walk, provided here as a final offering for anyone who has undertaken all twelve of the walks in this book, or is ready for something (even) more demanding.

Look closely at the OS South Pennines map, and it becomes apparent that a horseshoe of high ground, most of it about 1300–1650 ft (400–500 m) above sea level, stretches round north of Hebden Bridge. Inside this arc are enclosed all the tributaries and streams which together make up the waters of the Hebden Water and Colden rivers and which empty eventually into the River Calder. Beyond are other river systems, some ending up in the River Ribble, some in the River Aire.

Ranged along this arc are six of the Ordnance Survey's trig points: at Bride Stones (GR 932268), Hoof Stones Height (GR 913291), Boulsworth Hill (GR 930357), Stanbury Moor

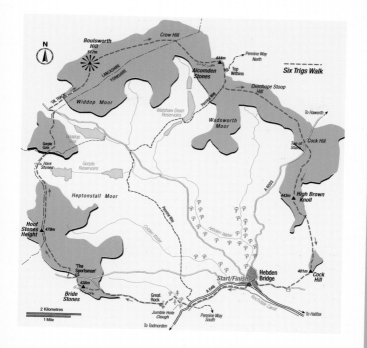

(GR 978357), High Brown Knoll (GR 009303) and Sheepstones (GR 014278). The task, therefore, is simply to put them together – to start at Hebden Bridge, visit all six trigs (either clockwise or anti-clockwise), and return to Hebden Bridge several hours later, tired but satisfied.

The idea for the Six Trigs was first floated late in 1999, in an article by this author in the outdoor magazine *TGO* (formerly *The Great Outdoors*). At the time, the point had to be made that the Six Trigs route crossed private land and would have to wait – at least for anyone not wanting to have to trespass – until the access legislation was in place. *TGO* kindly described the route as a 'soon-to-be classic'.

That time has now come, and the Six Trigs is available to all. The route is about the same length as a marathon (twenty-six miles/ forty-two kilometres), and although there is little climbing after the first pull-up from the Calder valley, the ground is in places hard going. Anyone attempting to walk it will probably take about ten hours to complete it (runners will be able to knock some hours off that time). The route includes the high moorland of Black Hameldon (featured in Walk 8), the Boulsworth Hill plateau (Walks

Black Clough

4 and 7), Crow Hill and the Alcomden Stones (Walk 5), Top Withens and Oxenhope Stoop (Walk 6), and High Brown Knoll (Walk 9).

There are no badges or certificates for completing the Six Trigs, and there is no organization to congratulate you on your achievement. What you will gain on the other hand is the pleasure of a hard day's walking, and the understanding that comes from a comprehensive introduction to some of the finest of the south Pennine moors.

Some further reading

Here is a small selection of books which will tell you more about the south Pennines area. Please note that not all of these books are still in print.

Paul Bennett, *The Old Stones of Elmet,* Capall Bann Publishing, 2001

K.J.S. Boughey and E.A. Vickerman, *Prehistoric Rock Art of the West Riding,* Yorkshire Archaeology 9, West Yorkshire Archaeology Service and English Heritage, 2003

Calderdale Way Association, *The Calderdale Way Guide,* third edition, CWA, 1997

Linda Croft, *John Fielden's Todmorden,* Tygerfoot Press, 1994

Peggy Hewitt, *These Lonely Mountains: a Biography of the Bronte Moors,* Springfield Books, 1985

Glyn Hughes, *Millstone Grit: a Pennine Journey,* Victor Gollancz, 1975

Ted Hughes, Fay Godwin, *Remains of Elmet* (republished as *Elmet*), Faber and Faber, 1979

Ilkley Archaeology Group, *Find the Past on Ilkley Moor: a Guide for Walkers*

Jim Jarratt, *The Watersheds Walk: a High-level Circuit of the Worth Valley,* Smith Settle, 1988

Bernard Jennings (ed.), *Pennine Valley,* Smith Settle, 1992

Arnold Kellett, *On Ilkla Mooar Baht 'At,* Smith Settle, 1998

Keith Parry, *Trans-Pennine Heritage: Hills, People and Transport,* David and Charles, 1981

Titus Thornber, *Seen on the Packhorse Tracks,* South Pennine Packhorse Trails Trust, 2002

Whiteley Turner, *A Spring-Time Saunter round and about Bronte Land,* 1912; new edition Rigg Publications, 1986

Stephen Welsh, *Cragg Vale: a Pennine Valley,* Pennine Desktop Publishing, 1993

The Country Code

An abbreviated version of the Country Code, launched in 2004 and supported by a wide range of countryside organizations including the Ramblers' Association, is given below.

Be safe – plan ahead and follow signs
Even when going out locally, it's best to get the latest information about where and when you can go; for example, your rights to enter some areas of open land may be restricted while work is being carried out, for safety reasons or during breeding seasons. Follow advice and local signs, and be prepared for the unexpected.

Leave gates and property as you find them
Please respect the working life of the countryside, as our actions can affect rural livelihoods, the safety and welfare of animals and people, and the heritage that belongs to all of us.

Protect plants and animals, and take your litter home
We have a responsibility to protect the countryside now and for future generations, so make sure you don't harm animals, birds, plants or trees.

Keep dogs under control
The countryside is a great place to exercise dogs, but it's every owner's duty to make sure their dog is not a danger or nuisance to farm animals, wildlife or other people.

Consider other people
Showing consideration and respect for other people makes the countryside a pleasant environment for everyone, whether they are at home, at work or at leisure.

INDEX

Index

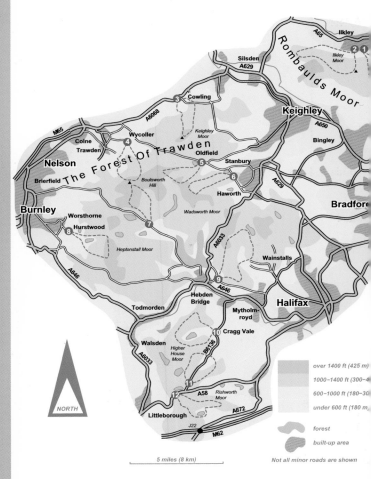

Rombaulds Moor

Ilkley
Ilkley Moor

Silsden
A629

Cowling

A6068

Wycoller

Keighley Moor

Keighley

A650

Bingley

Colne
Trawden

Oldfield

Stanbury

Bradfore

The Forest Of Trawden

Nelson

Brierfield

Boulsworth Hill

Haworth

Burnley

Worsthorne

Hurstwood

Wadsworth Moor

Heptonstall Moor

Wainstalls

A6033

A646

Halifax

Todmorden

Hebden Bridge

Mytholm-royd

Cragg Vale

Walsden

Higher House Moor

B6138

A6033

Rishworth Moor

A58

Littleborough

A672

J22
M62

NORTH

5 miles (8 km)

over 1400 ft (425 m)

1000–1400 ft (300–4

600–1000 ft (180–30

under 600 ft (180 m

forest

built-up area

Not all minor roads are shown